WHITEWASHING JULIA

Borgo Press Books by Frank J. Morlock

Castor and Pollux and Other Opera Libretti (Editor)
The Chevalier d'Éon and Other Short Farces (Editor)
Chuzzlewit
Congreve's Comedy of Manners
Crime and Punishment
Cyrano and Molière: Five Plays by or About Molière (Editor)
Falstaff (with Shakespeare, John Dennis, & William Kendrick)
Fathers and Sons
Herculaneum & Sardanapalus: Two Opera Libretti (Editor)
The Idiot
Isle of Slaves and Other Plays (Editor)
Jurgen
Justine
The Londoners & The Green Carnation: Two Plays
Lord Jim
The Madwoman of Beresina & Other Napoleonic Plays (Ed.)
Notes from the Underground
Oblomov
Old Creole Days
Outrageous Women: Lady Macbeth and Other Plays (Editor)
Peter and Alexis
The Princess Casamassima
A Raw Youth
Salammbô & Dido: Two Operas (Editor)
The Stendhal Hamlet Scenarios and Other Shakespearean Shorts from the French (Editor)
Two Voltairean Plays: The Triumvirate; and, Comedy at Ferney (Editor)
Whitewashing Julia and Other Plays
The Widow's Husband; and, Porthos in Search of an Outfit: Two Dumasian Comedies (Editor)
Zeneida & The Follies of Love & The Cat Who Changed into a Woman: Two Plays (Editor)

WHITEWASHING JULIA

AND OTHER PLAYS

FRANK J. MORLOCK

THE BORGO PRESS
MMXIII

WHITEWASHING JULIA

Copyright © 1981, 1984, 2001, 2013 by Frank J. Morlock

FIRST EDITION

Published by Wildside Press LLC

www.wildsidebooks.com

DEDICATION

For my good friend and doctor, Alan Segal

CONTENTS

WHITEWASHING JULIA 9
CAST OF CHARACTERS 10
THE PLAY 11
THE SEVEN CREAM JUGS; OR, IT RUNS IN THE
    FAMILY 85
CAST OF CHARACTERS 86
THE PLAY 87
VIOLENT ATTACHMENTS 127
CAST OF CHARACTERS 128
ACT I, Scene 1 129
ACT I, Scene 2 165
ACT II, Scene 3 174
ACT II, Scene 4 182
ABOUT THE AUTHOR 190

WHITEWASHING JULIA
BASED ON A PLAY OF THE SAME NAME BY HENRY ARTHUR JONES

CAST OF CHARACTERS

MR. WILLIAM STILLINGFLEET

MR. SAMWAYS

ELWIN PINKNEY

BEVIS PINKNEY

JULIA WREN

LADY PINKNEY

TRIXIE BLENKINSOP

MRS. FEWING

MRS. BENBOW

THE PLAY

The action takes place at a Church Bazaar, by the refreshment stand run by Lady Pinkney.

MRS. FEWING:

(entering) Yes! It was Julia! What shall we do?

LADY PINKNEY:

It will be impossible for us to know Julia unless the Berlin scandal is cleared up.

MRS. FEWING:

It's awkward for me. Still, she is my sister-in-law, and I can't not know her. And yet, I can't know her, can I?

LADY PINKNEY:

If we could only learn the truth. Samways is her cousin and her lawyer. And he must know all about it.

MRS. FEWING:

Of course he knows. But he always avoids the subject. When I heard Julia was coming back, I told Samways she would place me in a very awkward position.

LADY PINKNEY:

What did Samways say?

MRS. FEWING:

He asked me what I meant. I said I meant the scandal with the Duke. Then he asked me what I had heard. Then he asked me what everybody else had heard. I said everybody had heard all about the puff box, the dressing bag, and the tortoiseshell comb—and wasn't there a lace gown?

LADY PINKNEY:

I believe there was. Did Samways offer any explanation?

MRS. FEWING:

He said the Duchess was a mad woman, and had no doubt placed the articles there herself, on purpose, to make out a case against Julia. In fact, Samways pooh-poohs the whole affair.

LADY PINKNEY:

I'm afraid it's just one of those affairs that cannot be pooh-poohed. And now that Bevis has married into the Bishop's family—

MRS. FEWING:

I'm sure her dress comes from Paris. And she has dared to speak to the Bishop's wife.

LADY PINKNEY:

And did Mrs. Blenkinsop speak to her?

MRS. FEWING:

She was able to pass her to Mrs. Lane, the new school Mistress, who doesn't know Mrs. Wren's history.

LADY PINKNEY:

Do any of us know Mrs. Wren's history?

MRS. FEWING:

My dear Lady Pinkney, I gave you the whole story just as I had it from my agent. My agent was in Berlin a month after the scandal when everybody was full of it.

LADY PINKNEY:

(giving her a telegram) Here's something that may interest you. From my brother.

MRS. FEWING:

From Mr. Stillingfleet! Coming to Shanctonbury. Oh, Lady Pinkney, how can it interest me?

LADY PINKNEY:

My dear Caroline, I've always felt you were wrong to rebuff Bill.

MRS. FEWING:

Perhaps I was, but—

LADY PINKNEY:

Yes, I'm afraid Bill has been a very shocking rascal.

MRS. FEWING:

Do you think he has reformed?

LADY PINKNEY:

Now or never. He's just forty.

MRS. FEWING:

I think I should be more inclined now, then I was, to overlook any little manly weaknesses. Is he making a long stay?

LADY PINKNEY:

Until my husband returns from Australia. I shall lose no opportunity of letting Bill know he still has an opportunity of becoming a respectable member of society.

MRS. FEWING:

Thank you. I'm sure you won't compromise me.

(enter Bevis and his wife.)

BEVIS:

Mother, you will have to take an exceedingly firm attitude with regard to this lady.

MRS. BEVIS PINKNEY:

I simply declined to see her. I merely took up a box of handkerchiefs and studied them.

BEVIS:

Your behavior was admirable, Sophia. I will take care—and I'm sure my mother will take care, you are not subjected to such a disagreeable experience in the future.

(enter Samways, who pokes his head in and is about to withdraw.)

LADY PINKNEY:

(seeing him) Ah, Mr. Samways! Don't go! You're just the person we want. So your cousin, Mrs. Wren, is back in town?

SAMWAYS:

My second cousin. Yes, poor, dear girl.

BEVIS:

Does she intend to remain?

SAMWAYS:

For some time.

BEVIS:

Not under your advice?

SAMWAYS:

Well, I'm afraid I'm in some measure responsible. Everybody understands her natural delicacy.

BEVIS:

Delicacy?!!

SAMWAYS:

In staying away. But nobody believes these stories.

MRS. BEVIS:

Nobody?!

SAMWAYS:

Nobody who knows the circumstances.

LADY PINKNEY:

But, who does know the circumstances?

BEVIS:

Has Mrs. Wren—Julia—taken any steps to refute these stories?

SAMWAYS:

No, no, on my advice. Her reputation is sufficient answer.

MRS. FEWING::

Nobody's reputation could be sufficient to answer the puff box.

SAMWAYS:

Oh, Mrs. Fewing, I'm sure your reputation would be—

LADY PINKNEY:

Then you honestly believe those stories against Mrs. Wren are false?

SAMWAYS:

I can only say that were any defamatory story circulated against you or any lady present, I should defend you all with the same conviction. Eh! The weather seems a little threatening.

LADY PINKNEY:

But Samways you must see it is impossible for us to receive Mrs. Wren until this business is put to rest.

SAMWAYS:

Certainly. And if I can be of any assistance.

LADY PINKNEY:

Are you engaged for dinner tonight?

SAMWAYS:

No, but—

LADY PINKNEY:

We shall expect you at eight, and you shall give us the correct version of the whole affair so that we shall be able to take this very dear and much injured lady to our hearts and homes again. At eight precisely.

SAMWAYS:

Delighted, delighted.

(exit Samways.)

MRS. FEWING:

Samways means to help her wriggle out of it.

BEVIS:

We must take care she doesn't. We must insist upon evidence.

MRS. BEVIS:

I really don't see the need for evidence when one has already made up one's mind.

MRS. FEWING:

Quite so. Evidence merely confuses and unsettles one. It's so much better to have a firm, steady conviction from the first—and never change it.

LADY PINKNEY:

I wonder where Teddy is?

BEVIS:

We may be sure, mother, that wherever Teddy is, it is somewhere he ought not to be, and whatever he is doing, it is something he ought not to be doing.

MRS. BEVIS:

A pity he's the older brother. Come along, Bevis.

BEVIS:

You see it will be necessary to take a very firm attitude with Mrs. Wren.

(exit Bevis and Mrs. Bevis.)

(enter Julia.)

JULIA:

I beg your pardon. How d'ye do, Lady Pinkney?

LADY PINKNEY:

(bowing stiffly) How d'ye do?

JULIA:

Ah, Georgina.

MRS. FEWING:

(coldly) Hello, Julia.

JULIA:

I thought I could get a cup of tea. Perhaps, I'm too late?

LADY PINKNEY:

No. There's still a little left.

MRS. FEWING:

It's nearly cold.

JULIA:

I prefer it not too warm.

MRS. FEWING:

And very strong.

JULIA:

I like it rather strong.

MRS. FEWING:

It's really quite stewed.

JULIA:

I'm so thirsty, I don't mind if it's been stewed.

MRS. FEWING:

There's no cream and that's all the milk.

JULIA:

Thank you.

LADY PINKNEY:

(to Mrs. Fewing) I'll leave you to finish up here.

MRS. FEWING:

Very well, I'm coming in a moment.

LADY PINKNEY:

(to Julia) I hope you will have pleasant weather for your short stay in Shanctonbury.

(exit Lady Pinkney.)

JULIA:

You're looking wonderfully well, Georgina. I've been here a week and you haven't called?

MRS. FEWING:

My dear Julia, how could I? (curtly) More tea?

JULIA:

No.

MRS. FEWING:

If you want anything more, please help yourself.

JULIA:

Is anything the matter?

MRS. FEWING:

Matter? I warned you if you came back the whole town would cut you. You cannot imagine how embarrassing it is for me.

JULIA:

My dear Georgina, if it's embarrassing for you, what must it be for me?

MRS. FEWING:

But why have you come?

JULIA:

Nowhere else to go. I cannot afford to live overseas any more.

MRS. FEWING:

It isn't that I'm straitlaced. We were all willing to shut our eyes before. That was before the puff box. Especially as he was a royal!

JULIA:

But since the puff box—

MRS. FEWING:

My dear Julia!

(exit Mrs. Fewing. Julia puts the tea down with distaste. Enter Trixie Blenkinsop.)

TRIXIE:

Ah, there you are.

JULIA:

Trixie. But you know you mustn't see me unless Mrs. Blenkinsop knows.

TRIXIE:

She knows.

JULIA:

What?

TRIXIE:

And my uncle knows, too.

JULIA:

The Bishop knows you have come to see me. (joyously) My dear Trixie. (kissing her) How did you manage it?

TRIXIE:

Well, I was determined to see you. You know you can generally get what you want, if only you go on my plan.

JULIA:

What is your plan?

TRIXIE:

My old nurse said to me, "My cherub"—she used to call me her cherub—"My cherub," she said, "if you want your way in this world you must let folks see that you mean to scratch first, scratch hardest, and scratch longest. And then folks generally won't scratch you at all." (triumphantly showing her nails and blowing on them)

Nobody ever scratches me.

JULIA:

But you didn't scratch.

TRIXIE:

Oh, I had a row with Auntie.

JULIA:

My dear Trixie, you can't go through life having famous rows with everybody.

TRIXIE:

Why not? I always win. Actually, I love it. Auntie had hysterics and then, when Uncle came in, I had hysterics.

JULIA:

Well—?

TRIXIE:

Poor Uncle lifted up his hands to heaven. And so, you see, here

I am.

JULIA:

(gravely) I'm very sorry and very angry with you. (Trixie comes up winningly) No, Trixie, you know how much I love you, but I can never see or speak to you again.

TRIXIE:

(trying to embrace her) Oh, Julia.

JULIA:

What will your aunt think of me? What will the dear Bishop think of me? They will think I encourage you to come here.

TRIXIE:

Who cares?

JULIA:

Trixie!

TRIXIE:

Oh—forgive me.

JULIA:

You must go back at once and tell your aunt I was very angry with you for coming to me against her wish, and that I sent you to beg her pardon.

TRIXIE:

Beg her pardon! Not on your life!

JULIA:

Then our friendship is at an end.

TRIXIE:

Well, that's what they want anyway.

(exit Trixie in a fury. Samways enters.)

SAMWAYS:

Well? What did I tell you?

JULIA:

But have you explained it to them?

SAMWAYS:

No. Up to the present I have carefully avoided explanations, but tonight I am to dine with Lady Pinkney.

JULIA:

That will give you a splendid opportunity, won't it?

SAMWAYS:

To do what?

JULIA:

To prove to them how unfortunate I've been.

SAMWAYS:

Yes, yes. (gazing over his spectacles at her) But, how do we get over the puff box?

JULIA:

The puff box?

SAMWAYS:

And the other things?

JULIA:

You can't expect me to remember all the details!

SAMWAYS:

But the question is this: do we own up to the puff box—or do we deny the very existence of the puff box?

JULIA:

Well? What do you think?

SAMWAYS:

What do I think?

JULIA:

You're the lawyer. You surely don't expect me to teach you your business.

SAMWAYS:

My dear Julia, do let me explain to you once and for all the nature of evidence.

JULIA:

No, no, I hate technicalities.

SAMWAYS:

But if I'm to help you, I must know what line to take. Give me the exact particulars.

JULIA:

I have given you the exact particulars.

SAMWAYS:

Yes, but the exact particulars have never been quite the same. Let us make up our mind, once and for all, what the exact particulars are.

JULIA:

What ought I to do?

SAMWAYS:

Dish it up as well as you can. But tell her the complete story. Or at least a complete story.

JULIA:

Suppose—

SAMWAYS:

Yes?

JULIA:

Suppose I had a perfect answer to all these insinuations but, for urgent reasons, my lips were closed. What would you advise me to do?

SAMWAYS:

I should advise you to open them.

JULIA:

I see you don't believe in me.

SAMWAYS:

Now, now. What is the nature of this evidence you cannot reveal?

JULIA:

(mysteriously) Do you know anything about morganatic marriages?

SAMWAYS:

A little. Same as any other. It's binding. But the Duke was

already married. Give it up, my dear Julia! You'll get into it very deep if you don't.

JULIA:

But I'm in very deep water, clearly. Suppose there had been, I won't say a regular morganatic marriage, but something equivalent to a morganatic marriage. (Samways stares at her) It's hard when your own relations don't believe in you! (starts to cry)

SAMWAYS:

Julia, don't cry.

JULIA:

I've got to put in an appearance at the raffle! My lips are sealed.

(exit Julia trying to compose herself.)

SAMWAYS:

But Julia! (helplessly) Why is it women can never understand the nature of evidence?

(Bevis enters furtively.)

SAMWAYS:

(looking at him) Anything the matter?

BEVIS:

No. Er, Samways—

SAMWAYS:

Yes.

BEVIS:

If I wished to consult you—

SAMWAYS:

Certainly.

BEVIS:

It doesn't concern myself.

SAMWAYS:

Never does.

BEVIS:

A dear old friend.

SAMWAYS:

Always.

BEVIS:

This friend was betrayed into—a friendship with a very desirable undesirable young woman. And in his desperation, he came to me.

SAMWAYS:

Well?

BEVIS:

I promised to help him.

SAMWAYS:

How?

BEVIS:

To, ah pay the girl's mother. I arranged things and got them away to Australia.

SAMWAYS:

What then?

BEVIS:

I think I've just seen the mother. It would be a terrible blow to my wi—to my friend—if these women were to turn up again.

SAMWAYS:

(delicately) Was there any result of this friendship?

BEVIS:

(puzzled, then understanding) Result? No.

SAMWAYS:

Then what's disturbing you?

BEVIS:

Nothing.

SAMWAYS:

Have they your friend's letters?

BEVIS:

Not so stupid. No, not a scrap.

SAMWAYS:

Did he make her any promises before witnesses?

BEVIS:

I believe she doesn't even know his real name. He was most careful.

SAMWAYS:

Then, he's got nothing to fear, so far as I can see.

BEVIS:

A most unpleasant business. Yet it has been of some benefit to me. Taught me to be very strict in all such matters.

SAMWAYS:

Naturally. Where did you see the woman?

BEVIS:

Good Heavens!

SAMWAYS:

What is it?

BEVIS:

My Uncle.

SAMWAYS:

Bill,hHow are you? Welcome back!

(enter William Stillingfleet.)

STILLINGFLEET:

Ah, my dear Samways, how are you?

SAMWAYS:

First-rate.

STILLINGFLEET:

Bevis, my boy, how are you?

BEVIS:

Quite well, Thanks.

STILLINGFLEET:

And brother Teddy?

BEVIS:

Teddy is as usual. My brother and I have nothing in common.

STILLINGFLEET:

Let me see, you were married a few months ago; my congratulations! You must present me.

BEVIS:

Of course. Perhaps I may as well prepare you.

STILLINGFLEET:

No bad news, I hope?

BEVIS:

No, but everything was very lax in the old Bishop's time. My father-in-law, the present Bishop, and my mother-in-law, Mrs. Blenkinsop, have inaugurated a totally new regime.

STILLINGFLEET:

Ah! Not lax, eh?

BEVIS:

No, on the contrary. I needn't say we're delighted to see you.

STILLINGFLEET:

Thank you.

BEVIS:

You're going to stay some months with us?

STILLINGFLEET:

Well, yes. If the new regime is not too bracing.

BEVIS:

Of course, I don't wish to remind you of certain incidents that occurred during your former visits.

STILLINGFLEET:

Well then, don't remind me.

BEVIS:

Incidents I'm sure we all wish to see buried.

STILLINGFLEET:

I'm sure we do. Nobody more than myself. We'll bury them straight off, shall we? In fact, we'll cremate them.

(Samways at the counter with drink, chuckling.)

BEVIS:

In all seriousness, Uncle, in all sincerity, in all friendliness, I hope you'll allow me to give you a word of advice.

STILLINGFLEET:

Certainly.

BEVIS:

You may think me presumptuous.

STILLINGFLEET:

No! I'm sure, from the line you're taking, you're actuated by a genuine desire for my welfare, aren't you? Come now! Confess it!

BEVIS:

I am indeed.

STILLINGFLEET:

I was sure of it. Now go on!

BEVIS:

If I may give you a caution which you must allow is justified by certain incidents in your former visits.

STILLINGFLEET:

My dear boy, we cremated them some minutes ago.

BEVIS:

So far as possible.

STILLINGFLEET:

My dear Bevis, when you cremate a thing, cremate it and have done with it. Don't go raking amongst the dead ashes.

BEVIS:

In any case, we shall expect you to adopt the somewhat altered standard that now prevails in Shanctonbury.

STILLINGFLEET:

I will! I will! Nobody is more anxious to improve other people's morals than I am.

BEVIS:

I see you haven't changed, Uncle. I'm afraid you won't find your present visit a very congenial one.

(exit Bevis.)

STILLINGFLEET:

We shall see. (to Samways) That clammy young prig hasn't altered in the least. Just like his father. How has the other one turned out?

SAMWAYS:

Teddy? We've had a terrible time with Teddy.

STILLINGFLEET:

You mean the opera singer?

SAMWAYS:

Yes. Teddy would insist on marrying the girl. We had the Devil's own job to part them. At last Lord Pinkney dragged Teddy off to Australia, and I squared the girl with five thousand pounds.

STILLINGFLEET:

Teddy's back again, isn't he?

SAMWAYS:

Yes, poor Teddy! I like him! There's no vice in Teddy. He's only a damned silly sentimental idiot.

(enter Teddy.)

TEDDY:

I heard that Samways. You were talking about me.

SAMWAYS:

No—I—er—

TEDDY:

Oh yes, you were. I recognized the description.

SAMWAYS:

I'm—er, very sorry.

TEDDY:

(patting Samways) Don't fret, Samways, it's true. I am a damned silly sentimental idiot. (As Teddy turns to Stillingfleet, Samways beats a hasty, embarrassed retreat) Ah, Uncle Bill—how goes it?

STILLINGFLEET:

How are you, Teddy?

TEDDY:

A bit slack at present. I come to you, because being a bit of a black sheep yourself, eh?

STILLINGFLEET:

Well, off-white, brown.

TEDDY:

We black sheep ought to stick together. You don't know how the old lady rags me. And Bevis! He's a holy horror, Bevis. Well, I got back from Australia three months ago.

STILLINGFLEET:

What happened then?

TEDDY:

The old lady didn't kill the fatted calf for me, I assure you!

STILLINGFLEET:

No?

TEDDY:

Instead of trotting out the fatted calf, she trots out Miss Trixie Blenkinsop, the Bishop's niece. And Teddy is expected to worship the little beast and marry her.

STILLINGFLEET:

What does Teddy say to that?

TEDDY:

No, thank you. Bevis has married a Blenkinsop. One Bevis and one Blenkinsop are enough in any family. Besides, coming back on the boat from Australia, there was such a handsome girl.

STILLINGFLEET:

What?

TEDDY:

She appeals to me. She appeals to me.

STILLINGFLEET:

You're not thinking of it?

TEDDY:

No, no. It's this hole of a place and that Blenkinsop gang. A gruesome state of affairs. Have you ever been in love, Uncle

Bill?

STILLINGFLEET:

Scores of times.

TEDDY:

(disgusted) I asked for a little sympathy. (going off) Hush! The old lady! You won't tell her?

STILLINGFLEET:

No, Teddy, but—

TEDDY:

Honor! Hush!

(enter Lady Pinkney.)

LADY PINKNEY:

Ah, my dear Bill, I'm delighted. Don't go, Teddy!

STILLINGFLEET:

Ah, Madge, my darling. (kissing her) I'm very glad to see you.

LADY PINKNEY:

Teddy, where have you been all afternoon?

TEDDY:

I've been ruminating.

LADY PINKNEY:

But, you were told off to help Blenkinsop at their stall.

TEDDY:

With Trixie Blenkinsop? Thank you. I told my self off to scuttle.

LADY PINKNEY:

They're all waiting for you to help with the raffle.

TEDDY:

Let them wait. I've had just about enough of this Blenkinsop bevy. "Oh, for a lodge in some vast wilderness!"

(exit Teddy sulking.)

LADY PINKNEY:

That wretched boy! What shall I do with him? If only Bevis had been the elder!

STILLINGFLEET:

I am rather glad he's not.

LADY PINKNEY:

Really Bill! You're incorrigible. But I am glad to see you. You're earlier than we expected.

STILLINGFLEET:

I took the express. Well, Madge, you're looking wonderfully

young and charming.

LADY PINKNEY:

It must be my troubles and worries that preserve me. I hope you haven't come to add to them.

STILLINGFLEET:

Only with a view of making you still younger and more charming.

LADY PINKNEY:

No, Bill, I don't want any compliments. You're well over forty. Surely, you're not going to have any more escapades. I've trouble enough with the boys.

STILLINGFLEET:

Surely not Bevis?

LADY PINKNEY:

Oh, he's terribly strict. Anyway, however fond I am of you, and however much you may stand in need of my watchfulness, I've no time to look after you and keep you out of mischief.

STILLINGFLEET:

My dear Madge, as you say, I'm over forty, and I really believe I am now arriving at an age when I shall soon be able to care for myself and keep myself out of mischief.

LADY PINKNEY:

I hope so. That reminds me. We're likely to have something of a scandal in Shanctonbury.

STILLINGFLEET:

(enchanted) Indeed.

LADY PINKNEY:

Mrs. Wren has come back.

STILLINGFLEET:

Julia?

LADY PINKNEY:

You weren't in Shanctonbury at the time.

STILLINGFLEET:

Ah, yes. I remember. The Grand Duke. The puff box.

LADY PINKNEY:

Yes. Now, Bill, promise me you won't meet her.

STILLINGFLEET:

Now that was a most promising affair. Cat of a woman, the Duchess. I hear she worried the poor Duke into his grave.

LADY PINKNEY:

No, he died of German measles.

STILLINGFLEET:

I should like to know the real history of that puff box.

LADY PINKNEY:

Samways is dining with us tonight, and I intend to know everything. I've asked Mrs. Fewing.

STILLINGFLEET:

Poor Georgina! Do you remember, I proposed to Georgina four years ago? Lucky escape.— I mean for her.

LADY PINKNEY:

I don't think so. Georgina has seven thousand pounds a year. Now, Bill, think what a comfort it would be to us, if you would—

STILLINGFLEET:

Marry Georgina Fewing.

LADY PINKNEY:

Well, I don't wish to be premature. Still, consider the opportunity.

STILLINGFLEET:

To do what?

LADY PINKNEY:

To reform yourself, generally. Guiding my boys—

STILLINGFLEET:

Certainly. Don't mind doing any amount of general reformation. Why, only five minutes ago, I was giving the very best advice to Teddy.

LADY PINKNEY:

What about?

STILLINGFLEET:

His love affairs. Just a word: keep a very sharp watch on Teddy.

LADY PINKNEY:

Bill! Surely, he hasn't taken up with another one?

STILLINGFLEET:

Can't say. But keep a very sharp look out on Teddy.

LADY PINKNEY:

(aghast) There's another one. I feel sure there is. (Church bell rings in the distance) The bell for the Bishop's sermon. Will you come?

STILLINGFLEET:

I don't feel particularly in need of spiritual refreshment. But bodily! I haven't had any lunch.

LADY PINKNEY:

You'll find something here. I must go. Dinner at eight. (turning back, very imperatively) Bill, remember! You are not to know this Mrs. Wren.

STILLINGFLEET:

Of course not. Of course not!

(enter Trixie, excitedly, not seeing Lady Pinkney.)

TRIXIE:

Mrs. Wren, Mrs. Wren! I haven't gone yet.

LADY PINKNEY:

Miss Blenkinsop! I cannot believe my eyes.

TRIXIE:

Aunt and uncle know that I'm here.

LADY PINKNEY:

Trixie! How can you tell me such a dreadful story?

TRIXIE:

Oh, Mrs. Pinkney, I'm capable of anything. No one knows how abandoned and depraved I can be. But, bad as I am, I don't lie! And I allow no one to question my word.

LADY PINKNEY:

(seizing her hand) Come with me at once. I must see the Bishop and Mrs. Blenkinsop about this.

TRIXIE:

(pulling her hand loose) No! After what has just passed, I cannot be seen in public with you.

(exit Trixie.)

STILLINGFLEET:

That's the young lady you intend for Teddy?

LADY PINKNEY:

Yes.

STILLINGFLEET:

Won't she be rather a handful for him?

LADY PINKNEY:

My dear Bill, we must make haste and marry Teddy to somebody.

STILLINGFLEET:

Before he marries himself to a nobody.

LADY PINKNEY:

He simply has no sense of what is due to our position. I must run over to the bishop's and find out what is the meaning of her being with Mrs. Wren.

(exit Lady Pinkney.)

(enter Julia.)

JULIA:

I thought I heard somebody shrieking.

STILLINGFLEET:

We had a little scene with Miss Blenkinsop.

JULIA:

Trixie? Where is she?

STILLINGFLEET:

My sister has followed her to the Bishop's palace. Perhaps it will be better not to announce our engagement to my sister just for the time, eh?

JULIA:

I leave it all to you. Do it just when you think the right moment has come.

STILLINGFLEET:

It won't be today. Don't you think it would be better for us to—ah, satisfy the good people of Shanctonbury?

JULIA:

I wonder what would satisfy the good people of Shanctonbury. What would satisfy you?

STILLINGFLEET:

Have I ever seemed curious?

JULIA:

No. Then you are quite satisfied.

STILLINGFLEET:

Quite. Quite.

JULIA:

Well?

STILLINGFLEET:

Well?

JULIA:

What ought I to do?

STILLINGFLEET:

I think you ought to say.

JULIA:

Say what?

STILLINGFLEET:

Well, just enough to make people's minds easy about you.

JULIA:

Suppose that were difficult?

STILLINGFLEET:

Difficult?

JULIA:

Suppose, I only say, suppose. Suppose it were impossible?

STILLINGFLEET:

Then I would leave the matter entirely in your hands.

JULIA:

You would be satisfied to do that? For now and always?

STILLINGFLEET:

So far as my own happiness is concerned, I suspect nothing, I regret nothing! I guess nothing. I don't even want to know if there is anything to know.

JULIA:

You have the most complete confidence in me. I love being trusted.

STILLINGFLEET:

Cremation is best with dead loves. We will let the good people of Shanctonbury say and think what they please. We will say nothing. We understand each other. (they kiss)

(enter Teddy.)

TEDDY:

Hello again, Uncle Bill, Mrs. Wren. I saw the old lady going down the road.

STILLINGFLEET:

Yes, she's gone.

TEDDY:

I hope I have one true friend in Shanctonbury.

JULIA:

You have indeed.

TEDDY:

I should like to consult Mrs. Wren, privately if—

STILLINGFLEET:

You cannot do better. Trust her thoroughly, my boy.

JULIA:

Mr. Stillingfleet, you won't go very far— In case we need your advice.

(exit Stillingfleet.)

TEDDY:

You know, I'm in a situation that peculiarly demands the exercise of a little feminine tact and sympathy. There's nothing picks a man up like feminine sympathy. Especially when he's in the midst of events that may shape themselves into a kind of social revolution.

JULIA:

(alarmed) Social revolution! You're not going to head a social revolution?

TEDDY:

Yes, in a minor kind of way. With your aid and sympathy.

JULIA:

Oh, but I've no sympathy with social revolutions.

TEDDY:

Even one for your benefit?

JULIA:

My benefit? I'm sure no one ever benefits from a social revolution.

TEDDY:

You might.

JULIA:

I don't understand.

TEDDY:

With my help. And the help of some friends I am about to introduce into the neighborhood.

JULIA:

(doubtful) You're going to introduce some friends of yours?

TEDDY:

Yes. And I thought we might get up a nice little coterie of social outsiders and snap our fingers at the Bishop and the Blenkinsops.

JULIA:

But social outsiders don't form nice little coteries, do they? I'm sure they don't.

TEDDY:

You see, I'm going to get married.

JULIA:

What? And Lady Pinkney doesn't know?

TEDDY:

No.

JULIA:

You must tell Lady Pinkney at once.

TEDDY:

No. I brought the girl here on purpose to introduce her to you.

JULIA:

Well—of course, I should be delighted if Mr. Stillingfleet were present.

TEDDY:

I don't trust Uncle Bill. Oh—oh! Mother's coming. I'll clear out for a while.

(exit Teddy furtively. Enter Lady Pinkney.)

JULIA:

Dear Lady Pinkney. I was beginning to think my Shanctonbury friends had forgotten me.

LADY PINKNEY:

Oh no, dear. In fact, we've been thinking and talking a great deal about you.

JULIA:

Then I'm sure you've been thinking and saying all the kind things you possibly could.

LADY PINKNEY:

Now my dear Mrs. Wren, I'm going to have a little quiet, friendly talk on a subject of vital importance to you.

JULIA:

Yes, we women understand each other so much better than men understand us, don't we? For genuine sympathy, woman must always go to woman.

LADY PINKNEY:

Now, to return to our conversation. You are surprised old friends haven't called on you?

JULIA:

I did think it a little unkind. I must tell you I'm not responsible for Teddy's visits to me.

LADY PINKNEY:

(upset) My son Edward has been calling on you?

JULIA:

Yes. You didn't know?

LADY PINKNEY:

(very upset) Not a word. I think it most inconsiderate of him.

JULIA:

I told him so. And I asked him as a favor to me not to call again unless you knew.

LADY PINKNEY:

Thank you. Edward is a great trial to me.

JULIA:

He has a very sweet nature.

LADY PINKNEY:

Yes, yes. (hurriedly) May I ask how Edwin became acquainted with you?

JULIA:

Oh, but your brother presented him to me in London.

LADY PINKNEY:

(after choking) My dear Mrs. Wren. Now do let me warn you. In the strictest confidence, my brother is a most charming man, and I'm personally fond of him—

JULIA:

And he simply adores you.

LADY PINKNEY:

Yes, yes, But for your own sake let me beg you not to encourage his visits.

JULIA:

(enjoying herself) You think Mr. Stillingfleet is not, not quite, a nice acquaintance for me?

LADY PINKNEY:

Well, I won't say that. But he is the most erratic, impossible creature where women are concerned. I'm speaking solely in your interest, solely for your good.

JULIA:

I'm sure you are.

LADY PINKNEY:

Now please, let my brother plainly understand that he will not be welcome in the future.

JULIA:

Certainly, if you wish it. But I've so few friends—

LADY PINKNEY:

I was certainly not aware, either, that Miss Blenkinsop had been visiting you. (Julia says nothing) It was quite against my wish.

JULIA:

Yes, so she said.

(enter Bevis and Samways.)

BEVIS:

This is an extraordinary story about my brother.

SAMWAYS:

Yes, curious, isn't it?

BEVIS:

Mother! Teddy is going to marry another one of them. He's just told us.

LADY PINKNEY:

What? What is to be done? What would Pinkney say?

JULIA:

Dear Lady Pinkney, will you think me intrusive if I make a suggestion?

LADY PINKNEY:

No, no. When did you first know of this?

JULIA:

Only a moment before you came. Let me help you out of this difficulty.

LADY PINKNEY:

How?

JULIA:

If I were you, I should not oppose this marriage.

LADY PINKNEY:

Not oppose it?!!

JULIA:

Not for the moment. You must gain time. Tell them that the marriage cannot take place until Lord Pinkney returns from Australia. That will take six months.

LADY PINKNEY:

My dear Mrs. Wren.

JULIA:

I will suggest they take a trip to the continent. I'll send Meade with them. A great deal may happen in six months.

LADY PINKNEY:

It's a great scheme. I congratulate you.

JULIA:

Shall I suggest it to them?

LADY PINKNEY:

Well, there could be no harm.

JULIA:

Well, leave it to me; I'll try to get them to accept it.

LADY PINKNEY:

Thank you very much. Dear Mrs. Wren, I'll leave the matter in your hands.

JULIA:

(going) I'll be right back.

LADY PINKNEY:

Your nearest way will be through the conservatory.

JULIA:

Oh, I know quite well. You forget I used to be a frequent visitor here.

(exit Julia.)

(Lady Pinkney sinks exhausted into a chair. Stillingfleet enters after a moment.)

LADY PINKNEY:

Ah, Bill, Mrs. Wren is being very helpful about Teddy.

STILLINGFLEET:

Is she?

LADY PINKNEY:

I must make her a very handsome acknowledgment. And then it would be a great relief to everybody if she would leave Shanctonbury, eh?

STILLINGFLEET:

I don't think so, After all this help she's been, I should have thought you would wish her to stay near you.

LADY PINKNEY:

Personally, I should be delighted. But it's useless for her to think of living in Shanctonbury unless she clears up the puff box. Meantime, what acknowledgment do you think—?

STILLINGFLEET:

It's difficult to say.

LADY PINKNEY:

We certainly owe her a large debt of gratitude.

STILLINGFLEET:

A present would be a very grave mistake.

LADYPINKNEY:

Why?

STILLINGFLEET:

It would look as if you thought her services could be bought and paid for.

LADY PINKNEY:

Well, what!

STILLINGFLEET:

It's a dilemma, but I think I can help you out of it.

LADY PINKNEY:

How?

STILLINGFLEET:

I don't think you know how attached you are to Mrs. Wren. As for myself—

LADY PINKNEY:

Bill!

STILLINGFLEET:

In fact, I've been thinking over the good advice you've been giving me for years past about settling down.

LADY PINKNEY:

Bill!

STILLINGFLEET:

That's the best of me. I do take good advice. Not all the time perhaps. Good advice shouldn't be taken recklessly, should it? No. It seems to roll off me like water off a duck, but all the while, Madge, it's making a deep impression on me. Or rather, in me. I'm taking it internally. That dear good sister of mine. She's right after all. Now, where can I find a woman—?

LADY PINKNEY:

(much alarmed) Bill!

STILLINGFLEET:

A woman of refinement?

LADY PINKNEY:

Bill, you're not going to marry Mrs. Wren!

STILLINGFLEET:

You see, you recognized her description in a moment! Now congratulate me.

LADY PINKNEY:

Bill, this is too bad of you! If you marry Mrs. Wren, it will make Shanctonbury quite impossible for me!

(Bill looks undisturbed by this prospect; some might think quite enchanted with the idea.)

(enter Julia.)

JULIA:

Trixie and Edward just raced off to the Bishop's palace on the best of terms with each other. I'm sure I can easily lead them into a real attachment. (looking at Lady Pinkney) Is anything the matter?

LADY PINKNEY:

No, my brother has just told me.

STILLINGFLEET:

She's naturally a little surprised to hear of our engagement. Such a dear sympathetic creature. (Lady Pinkney is gasping, ready to burst) Oh, don't deny it, my dear!

LADY PINKNEY:

(after composing herself bravely, frigidly) May I ask how this has come about?

STILLINGFLEET:

Oh, we met in London and studied Botany together.

LADY PINKNEY:

Botany? You have been studying Botany? (under her breath) Anatomy, more likely!

STILLINGFLEET:

Er, yes. A few rudiments. Do you know, Madge, I actually didn't know the names of our commonest wildflowers. Bugloss, Bladder Campion, Sticklewort. Sticklewort, or Stipplewort?

Still don't. It's disgraceful for a man to arrive at my age and not know the names of the simplest wildflowers.

LADY PINKNEY:

Stipplewort! Sticklewort! You'll drive me mad with your, your An—Botany! (she rushes out)

JULIA:

I'm afraid we've made her angry.

STILLINGFLEET:

Madge will get over it. She's really not a prude.

JULIA:

No?

STILLINGFLEET:

Not in the least, by nature, that is. She actually has a skeleton or two in her closet.

JULIA:

Lady Pinkney? Not possible.

STILLINGFLEET:

Something like a family crypt if it were ever to be dug up.

JULIA:

(laughing) You mustn't say things like that.

STILLINGFLEET:

She was bidding fair to outstrip her older brother, and would have too, by Jove, if she hadn't fallen in love with Pinkney, and immolated herself on the altar of respectability.

JULIA:

You are making things up.

STILLINGFLEET:

Word of a gentleman. I could tell you some things—

JULIA:

You mustn't tell me your sister's secrets.

STILLINGFLEET:

Somehow, I feel I really must. For instance, in Venice there was the famous gondola incident.

JULIA:

Hush!

(Stillingfleet is warming up to relate the story with great relish when Bevis enters looking very serious.)

BEVIS:

(to Julia) Will you allow me a few moments with my uncle?

JULIA:

Certainly. (to Stillingfleet) Whatever happens, don't let me bring discord into your family.

STILLINGFLEET:

Oh, you shan't. (to Bevis after Julia leaves) Now, my boy—

BEVIS:

I cannot say that I am surprised, remembering certain incidents in your former career.

STILLINGFLEET:

My dear Bevis, we cremated 'em.

BEVIS:

I did not, as you term it, cremate them.

STILLINGFLEET:

(sharply) Well, I did.

BEVIS:

After those incidents I cannot say that any action of yours would cause me any great surprise or concern.

STILLINGFLEET:

No? I thought you showed just a little too much concern.

BEVIS:

On account of our family, yes. On account of my dear mother, and wife, yes. On account of the unpleasantness all around that must attend this most ill-advised step, yes. But on your account, no.

STILLINGFLEET:

Quite thrown me over, eh? Quite washed your hands of me?

BEVIS:

I think you might, for once, drop your habit of turning everything into a jest. Surely, you must see this as a serious moment.

STILLINGFLEET:

It is. And if you and your wife object to sit at the table with the lady who is to be my wife, I advise you to hurry across to the Bishop's palace and join their party.

BEVIS:

I wasn't thinking of dinner.

STILLINGFLEET:

Well, I was. Now, shall we let the matter rest?

BEVIS:

I cannot allow the matter to rest. I have never felt so thoroughly upset in the whole course of my life.

STILLINGFLEET:

Upset at what?

BEVIS:

At the painful prospect of Mrs. Wren being introduced into our family. Now, my dear Uncle, I do beg you to realize what it is you are doing. It's not yet too late.

STILLINGFLEET:

My dear Bevis, it's too late. Too late even for sermonizing about it.

BEVIS:

But reflect? What will be the result of this undesirable alliance? What does my mother say? How am I to regard it? Do you intend to reside amongst us? You will find it impossible. What do you suppose, what do you suppose will be the effect in Shanctonbury?

STILLINGFLEET:

I hope I shall never willingly shock or offend my neighbors. But I will allow neither you nor your mother nor anyone else to dictate to me whom I shall marry, or where I shall live when I have married.

BEVIS:

(incensed) Very well! I don't know what mother's feelings or intentions may be, but speaking for myself and my wife's family, I must tell you frankly we shall not countenance this marriage; we shall not recognize you or your wife in any way. We shall let all our neighbors plainly see how we regard you, and if you continue to live in Shanctonbury—

(enter Mrs. Benbow.)

MRS. BENBOW:

I beg your pardon for intruding. Oh, Mr. Stillingfleet, how d'ye do?

STILLINGFLEET:

Hello.

(Bevis tries to hide his face.)

MRS. BENBOW:

I'm looking for Lady Pinkney.

STILLINGFLEET:

This is Lady Pinkney's son.

MRS. BENBOW:

Teddy! Well, my business is with him as well. Oh, it's not Teddy.

BEVIS:

What do you want with me? I've paid you, haven't I?

MRS. BENBOW:

(surprised) Mr. Brown!

STILLINGFLEET:

Brown!

BEVIS:

I will have nothing to do with you. I—ah— (to Stillingfleet) She must be some impostor!

(enter Samways.)

SAMWAYS:

Ah, Mrs. Benbow.

BEVIS:

(grabbing Samways and whispering) One moment, Samways.

SAMWAYS:

(after a hurried consultation) All right. Leave it to me. Come this way, Mrs. Benbow.

MRS. BENBOW:

Of course. (to Bevis) Mr. Brown.

(exit Samways and Mrs. Benbow.)

STILLINGFLEET:

Old acquaintances.

BEVIS:

No, at least— Perhaps you think this affair requires an explanation.

STILLINGFLEET:

Not a bit, my dear lad. If you're in a mess, take my advice, don't explain to anybody how you got there, but quietly pick yourself up, wipe your boots and say no more about it. Now, can I lend you a helping hand?

BEVIS:

In what way? I'm not in any mess.

STILLINGFLEET:

Glad to hear it.

BEVIS:

When my past actions are examined, I shall have nothing to be ashamed of.

STILLINGFLEET:

I'm sure you won't. We shall learn a great deal that will redound to your credit.

BEVIS:

I don't say that—

STILLINGFLEET:

Ah, that's your modesty. You befriended that poor young lady and now stand here shaking with fright that your good charitable actions should become known, and blazed abroad in Shanctonbury. Isn't that right, eh! (Shaking Bevis good humoredly)

BEVIS:

(ghastly with fright) Uncle—I'll tell you everything.

STILLINGFLEET:

My dear Bevis, I don't wish to know.

BEVIS:

I'd better tell you in case any garbled account of it should become public. My only wish is to spare my dear mother and wife the pain of hearing anything that would destroy their ideal of me.

STILLINGFLEET:

All for the sake of others.

BEVIS:

I've tried to set a very high standard.

STILLINGFLEET:

All for the sake of others.

BEVIS:

That woman has no possible claim on me.

STILLINGFLEET:

No?

BEVIS:

Not morally.

STILLINGFLEET:

No?

BEVIS:

When I was at Oxford, I was betrayed into a very undesirable friendship. Really betrayed into it.

STILLINGFLEET:

I've had that happen so many times. I sympathize. Go on.

BEVIS:

But I very soon conquered.

STILLINGFLEET:

Brave boy!

BEVIS:

I got them out of the country to Australia, by paying a considerable sum. That's really all. I cannot imagine why they are here. (pause) Uncle, you won't misunderstand me?

STILLINGFLEET:

How?

BEVIS:

At first sight I might appear a hypocrite.

STILLINGFLEET:

Oh, not at all. Oh, no!

BEVIS:

No, I'm really not.

STILLINGFLEET:

Say no more. So far as I'm concerned, it's past. But there's someone who is very dear to me—

BEVIS:

Mrs. Wren! I fear I have been very mistaken in my estimate of Mrs. Wren.

STILLINGFLEET:

You will please let that be known.

BEVIS:

Oh, yes. To everybody.

STILLINGFLEET:

Yes, do, do. You're good at explanations.

BEVIS:

We shall receive her ourselves, and if she is received by us, I don't think you need have any doubt.

STILLINGFLEET:

Then I'll leave all the explaining to you.

BEVIS:

Yes, if Samways—

(enter Samways.)

SAMWAYS:

(rubbing his hands) That's settled. The lady leaves Shanctonbury tomorrow and we shall have no further trouble with her. (To Bevis) Your friend Mr. Brown need have no further anxiety.

BEVIS:

Whew! Thank you so much.

SAMWAYS:

The Teddy matter is settled, too. She can't very well pretend to innocence over the matter after having been involved with Mr. Bee—Mr. Brown.

(enter Julia.)

BEVIS:

(advancing cordially to her) My dear, dear Mrs. Wren. I very much regret there has been any misunderstanding between us and I hope we shall be good friends in the future. (offering his hand)

JULIA:

(nonplussed) I shall be delighted, but— (looking at Stillingfleet for an explanation, he merely nods and winks) but— (shaking Bevis's hand) Delighted.

(enter Trixie, followed by Lady Pinkney.)

LADY PINKNEY:

I wish never to have anything more to do with Trixie!

TRIXIE:

There! What did I tell you?

JULIA:

But Lady Pinkney, she is very sorry and has come to ask your forgiveness. Trixie.

TRIXIE:

(in a quick, hard, perfunctory, impertinent tone) I beg your pardon.

JULIA:

No, Trixie! Not in that tone.

TRIXIE:

(a shade softer) I beg your pardon, Lady Pinkney.

(Lady Pinkney remains cold and severe.)

TRIXIE:

(loud) I BEG YOUR PARDON, LADY PINKNEY!

JULIA:

Trixie! Trixie!

TRIXIE:

Well, what can I do? I beg your pardon, I beg your pardon, beg your pardon, beg your pardon, beg your pardon, beg your pardon, beg your pardon, beg your pardon, beg your pardon, beg your pardon, beg your pardon!

There!

JULIA:

I'm sorry Lady Pinkney, it is I who have to beg your pardon for having brought this rude, naughty girl to you. Will you please forgive me. (sternly to Trixie) Trixie, you might have spared me this!

TRIXIE:

(penitent) I'm very sorry, Lady Pinkney, I beg your pardon! I really mean it this time. Will you please forgive me?

LADY PINKNEY:

I forgive you, Trixie.

BEVIS:

How much better it is to be guided by the experience gained from our past follies.

STILLINGFLEET:

How much better still, never to commit any folly at all. To be always wise and judicious like you, eh, Bevis?

BEVIS:

I can't say I've never committed any folly or mistake.

STILLINGFLEET:

Oh, I think you might.

BEVIS:

But, I can honestly say that my past mistakes have really improved my character.

STILLINGFLEET:

Ah, now there's the danger of a character like yours. You go on improving it until it becomes a standing menace to all your neighbors. For the sake of us poor sinners, don't improve it any further.

BEVIS:

I wish you wouldn't jest about these things. (to his mother) Uncle William has explained everything to me most satisfactorily, and for my part, I shall dine with Mrs. Wren.

LADY PINKNEY:

I don't understand.

BEVIS:

You may be quite sure, mother, that I have thoroughly satisfied myself.

LADY PINKNEY:

But the puff box.

BEVIS:

I will not repeat scandal. Be satisfied that I am satisfied.

LADY PINKNEY:

Bevis. (they confer apart)

JULIA:

Do tell me! What did you tell him about me?

STILLINGFLEET:

Nothing.

JULIA:

Nothing?

LADY PINKNEY:

(emerging from the conference with a cordial smile) Oh, if Bevis is satisfied, I am more than satisfied. Everything is explained.

STILLINGFLEET:

Everything.

LADY PINKNEY:

I always knew the puff box was a pure myth. Yes, you acted very wisely, Julia, in saying nothing. I always said so.

CURTAIN

THE SEVEN CREAM JUGS; OR, IT RUNS IN THE FAMILY
A ONE-ACT PLAY BASED ON A STORY BY SAKI

CAST OF CHARACTERS

A SERVANT

PETER PIGEONCOTE

LADY ELEANOR PIGEONCOTE

WILFRED PIGEONCOTE, Peter's cousin

THE PLAY

A contemporary drawing room.

A large, ornate room filled with cardboard boxes in gift wrapping. Most of the boxes, large and small, have been opened, and the gifts give the room a joyous air.

A servant enters laden with more gifts, and dumps them on a couch, shrugs, and leaves.

Enter Peter Pigeoncote, middle-aged, distinguished-looking, very solid and formal. He stumbles over some boxes and utters an oath.

Peter

Break your neck with all these damn fool wedding gifts.

(Peter kicks a box furiously. Lady Eleanor has entered behind him, and, the perfect lady, she corrects her husband's crudity.)

Eleanor

Peter, I wish you wouldn't swear like that. The guests will hear you.

Peter

Damn the guests!

Eleanor (warningly)

Peter!

Peter

Oh, very well. It's a fine thing if a man can't express himself in his own house after nearly breaking his ankle, and on his daughter's wedding day. Freedom, I say freedom, no longer exists in these benighted isles.

Eleanor

Oh, Peter. She's so beautiful.

Peter (complacently)

Takes after me, of course.

Eleanor

Wretch!

Peter

She certainly has cleaned up. (surveying the gifts) Look at all this silver. (he takes up a gorgeous silver pot) Must be worth hundreds.

Eleanor

She's got six others just like it.

Peter

Very nice. I suppose we can't sell them, can we?

Eleanor

Peter, how can you?

Peter

Not all of them. She could keep one. Might help pay for this bash.

Eleanor

Peter, you're a terrible man.

Peter

Precisely the reason I married you, my dear. I was the ideal husband.

Eleanor

Stop being a tease.

Peter

After all, (musingly) I am a Pigeoncote, and it is well known that we Pigeoncotes are a disreputable lot.... In fact, disreputability is our principal claim to fame. (wryly) We are a nice lot.

Eleanor

Well, I admit that having a kleptomaniac as head of the family is a rather dubious distinction.

Peter

Yes, it was rather inconsiderate of Uncle Arthur to die and leave his estate to Wilfred the Snatcher.

Eleanor

I can't understand how Uncle Arthur could do such a thing. After all, there were several other members of the family more nearly related to Uncle Arthur than the Snatcher.

Peter

Like all Pigeoncotes, Uncle Arthur had a perverse sense of humor. He always liked to épater le bourgeois. He's probably up there (pointing heavenwards) thumbing his nose at us all.

Eleanor

I still think it must have been a mistake. He had three nephews named Wilfred. He was just confused.

Peter

It's a possibility. Wilfred has been a baptismal weakness in the family since the time of Wilfred the Conqueror.

Eleanor

That shows the danger of adhering to ancient traditions.

Peter

Please don't be so defensive because your family can only trace its lineage to the reign of Richard Lionheart.

Eleanor

Don't be ridiculous, my dear. I just think it's awful for you to be passed over in favor of a kleptomaniac.

Peter

Well, it's a minor failing. The Snatcher is perfectly undistinguished in every other respect. Besides, I'm told he lacks the taste of a connoisseur. Anything portable, Wilfred will take. In every other respect Wilfred is quite harmless and respectable. Doesn't even disgrace himself with women, like Uncle Arthur.

Eleanor

I suppose he won't show up for the wedding, now that he's the heir?

Peter

We can hardly expect him to, in view of the frigid way we treated him when he was a prospective nobody. I don't think we've set eyes on him since he was twelve.

Eleanor

Well, after all, there was a perfectly good reason. A person with his failing is not the sort one wants around the house.

Peter

Absolutely. Still, I can appreciate that he might not sympathize with our point of view.

Eleanor

But, if he came, he might give Diana the perfect gift.

Peter

I should prefer not having to worry if it were paid for. Besides, we would have to worry that he might steal one we've received already.

Eleanor

Peter, please don't use such a crude word to describe Wilfred's failing.

Peter

I'm afraid I was always taught to call a spade a spade. As I recall, we always had to search his luggage whenever he was a guest, to make sure he hadn't taken anything "by mistake." It would be rather more embarrassing now that he's full grown and the head of the family.

Eleanor

That is still a drawback, but one would like to make the acquaintance of the head of the family, and have him bestow his blessing on Diana. Besides, having money will make all the difference.

Peter

Poverty is no crime, but money excuses it, eh?

Eleanor

Certainly not. Peter, don't be obtuse. You know perfectly well what I mean. If he has money, all suspicion of a sordid motive disappears.

Peter

Lots of things disappear when Wilfred is around. Not just motives.

Eleanor

Don't be so cynical. It would be nice, you know...for Diana's wedding.

Peter

You know it killed his mother. Aunt Margaret was a fine old lady. Died of chagrin when he was fifteen. He was caught red-handed trying to steal a ring when he was presented at court.

(The servant enters with a telegram on a salver. She presents it to Peter, who takes it and reads it. The servant exits.)

Peter

This is a surprise. Here's a telegram from Wilfred saying he's passing through and would like to stop by and pay his respects. Must be the Snatcher.

Eleanor

How do you know it's the Snatcher? It might be the Gunner or the Attaché?

Peter

Not very likely. Wilfred the Gunner is with his regiment, east of Suez somewhere, and Wilfred the Attaché is in Burma or Thailand. No, the Snatcher is the only Wilfred Pigeoncote left in England.

Eleanor

Good gracious! This is rather an awkward time to have someone with his failing in the house. (looking at all the presents) I'm sure I'll be a nervous wreck.

Peter

I thought you were just saying you wanted him to come.

Eleanor

But, that was before I knew for sure he was coming, and seriously considered the complications.

Peter

It will be an interesting test of your theories.

Eleanor (aghast)

But, I don't even know for sure what we've got yet.

Peter

Lock them up.

Eleanor

But, we can't. He's sure to want to see them.

Peter

Tell him "no," he can't see them.

Eleanor

We can't do that.

Peter

Why not? We used to lock things up when he came before.

Eleanor

But, he's the head of the family now.

Peter

I fail to see how that alters things. He's still a thief.

Eleanor (sharply)

Peter! I will not have you use such language about Wilfred.

Peter (annoyed)

Very well. Kleptomaniac.

Eleanor (evenly)

No, Peter, he's afflicted. And one shouldn't mention an affliction, or call attention to it. We must pretend we are not aware of his affliction. That's good manners.

Peter (mumbling)

We must pretend we are not aware of his affliction. (shouting) So, we let him steal what he wants—is that it?

Eleanor (hesitating)

N-n-n-no. But, these practiced kleptomaniacs...I mean. (unable to think of a euphemism) Damn. Anyway, they're so clever.

Peter

We must keep a sharp lookout, that's all.

Eleanor

I'll die if he suspects we are watching him.

Peter

I'll die before I let him steal something. For God's sake, Eleanor, just because he's got money now, you're afraid to offend him.

Eleanor

I am not afraid to offend him. I'd just rather not, that's all. But, it's going to be difficult. I suppose we could hide some of the more expensive presents.

Peter

Kleptomaniacs have a genius for ferreting out the ones that are hidden. They know that something hidden is something highly prized.

Eleanor

This is such a dilemma.

(Enter servant with a salver which she presents to Peter. He removes a card, and the servant exits. Peter stares at the card.)

Peter

Good God, he's here already. This is his card.

(Lady Eleanor snatches one of the presents and rushes about the room, looking for a hiding place. First, she selects one place, then abandons it in favor of another. Nothing proves satisfactory. Peter watches her in consternation. He wants to say something, hesitates, and finally speaks in exasperation.)

Peter

Eleanor, stop behaving like an ass. We simply must see it through.

(Enter Wilfred. He is a tall, distinguished-looking young man, elegantly dressed. He also has elegant manners. He is quite at his ease.)

Wilfred

Evening, Cousin Peter, Lady Eleanor. I'll bet I arrived almost as soon as my telegram.

Peter

Er, yes, Wilfred. We just got it.

Wilfred

That's the way I planned it. I didn't want you to make any special preparations.

(Lady Eleanor, trying to conceal the presents she still has in her hands from his sight, struggles to keep facing him throughout the remainder of the scene.)

Eleanor

You—er—succeeded in preventing us from making any special preparations.

Peter (aside)

Clever devil. (aloud) Devilish clever of you, Wilfred.

Wilfred (looking at the presents, which he begins to touch)

I say. What a stash of loot. Cousin Diana is really doing well for herself.

(During the remainder of the scene Wilfred resembles nothing so much as a frolicking chipmunk into an acre of nuts. He goes from one present to another with lightning speed and short attention span. Every time he touches one, Peter lurches toward him to grab it away from him, but is checked by an imperious sign from Lady Eleanor. Peter relaxes a little, but not much, under a quelling stare from his wife.)

Wilfred (picking one up)

Let me see, what is this? (picking up another) This is cute, too. (he moves to another present) I've never seen one of these before. (moving on) Very nice. (moving on) Diana must be so pleased. (pause) You mustn't think I'm rude. I just can't resist looking at someone else's presents.

(Peter and Lady Eleanor exchange a glance. Peter again renews his vigilance, this time with less resistance from Lady Eleanor.)

Wilfred

I am so glad I could come. I didn't think I'd be able to get away.

Eleanor

Yes, we're surprised to you could make it.

Wilfred

I never miss an opportunity like this, if I can help it. Not for anything. (looking around)

Peter

I dare say.

Wilfred (fondling a present)

Lucky girl, Diana. Wouldn't mind having one of these myself.

Peter

I expect not.

Wilfred

But, I don't propose to get married to do it.

Peter

I'll say.

Wilfred

So needless.

Peter

Yes.

Wilfred

Been years since I've seen you. Just a boy then. But, I've grown up a lot. Bet you didn't recognize me.

Peter

Didn't really.

Eleanor

No, you don't look much the same. You've improved, though. Hasn't Wilfred improved, Peter?

Peter

Oh, yes. Much more clever than he used to be.

Wilfred (to Eleanor)

Give us a hug, for old times' sake, Lady Eleanor.

(Lady Eleanor desperately tries to hide the present she is holding.)

Wilfred

Say, what's that your holding?

Eleanor

Oh, just a silly present.

Wilfred

Here, let me see that.

Eleanor

Oh, no. You wouldn't be interested. It's just a silver dish.

Wilfred

I'm an expert on silver. I have quite a collection, you know.

Eleanor (trying to say something, but choking)

Hgghhh.

Wilfred (patting her on the back)

Here, here, old girl, let me take that. (taking the dish) Peter, better get Cousin Eleanor a glass of water.

(Peter exits backward, facing Wilfred. Wilfred does not notice, so absorbed is he in the present.)

Wilfred (examining the present)

Very elegant, Cousin. The workmanship is of the very highest quality. This is a real collector's item.

(Peter returns with the water.)

Peter (to Eleanor)

Didn't take my eyes off him.

Wilfred

What say, Peter?

Peter

I say I can't keep my eyes off this gift.

Wilfred

Can't blame you. (still holding the gift) Do you have any place to lock this stuff up?

Eleanor (confused)

Er, no, we'll just lock the doors to the drawing room.

Wilfred (expertly)

Not very safe. A thief could pick that lock in no time. Take that from me. I've got a little experience in this sort of thing. Why, I'd have no trouble with it myself.

(Lady Eleanor and Peter exchange a pregnant look.)

Peter

You seem to have developed quite a bit of expertise.

Wilfred

You ought to hire a guard. Have you got one already, perhaps?

Peter

No, until you came, the thought never crossed my mind.

Wilfred

A pity. It would be a shame if you woke up in the morning, and found all this stuff gone.

Peter

Yes, it would. I shan't let that happen. I shall sleep on the couch myself. (with significant emphasis) With my gun.

Wilfred

You keep weapons about the house? That's good to know.

Peter

Yes, they're useful—for shooting snipe and (significantly) sneaks.

Wilfred

That's a capital idea. I'd be glad to do it for you, if you like.

Peter (aside)

I'll bet you would. (aloud) I couldn't let you do that. You're a guest.

Wilfred

But, you must be awfully tired. I'd be glad to help you out any way I can.

Eleanor

I know you would, but Peter is quite inflexible in observing the rules of hospitality. Aren't you, Peter?

Peter

I'm inexorable.

Wilfred

Just as you think best. Only trying to help out.

Eleanor

It's very kind of you. Let me show you the other gifts.

(Peter makes signs for her not to do it, but Lady Eleanor ignores him. Eleanor speaks to Peter as Wilfred takes a present to the light to examine it.)

Eleanor

Our only hope of stopping him is to make him think we suspect nothing.

Peter

Bravo! Bright girl.

Eleanor (to Wilfred)

Nice, useful gifts. A few duplicates, of course.

Peter

Seven cream jugs.

Wilfred

You'd never miss one, would you?

Eleanor

Oh, we'd know immediately. People do have such limited imaginations, don't they?

Wilfred

It's a shame to give a duplicate. (musing) Makes a person look foolish.

(Although they are trying to be nonchalant, Peter and Lady Eleanor grab the gifts back from Wilfred after he touches them.)

Wilfred

Of course, you could just dispose of some of them, and say they were stolen.

Peter (nervously)

I suppose we could do that. I had thought of selling them. All, but one set.

Eleanor (anxiously)

Did you give me back the dish? This is its place, here.

Wilfred

Sorry, I put it down by the tea service. (handling another object)

Eleanor

Could I have that, again? I have to label who it comes from, before I quite forget. (clutching it impulsively)

Wilfred (giving it back)

Oh, certainly. Well, I'd better go see Diana, and then get to bed. (looking at his watch) It's been a long day. See you in the morning.

(Wilfred goes out gaily. The minute the door closes behind him, Lady Eleanor and Peter pounce on the gifts, trying to see if anything is missing.)

Eleanor

He's taken something, I just know it.

Peter

I fancy by his manner there was something up. "Better go see Diana," indeed. The scoundrel. Do you miss anything?

Eleanor

How can I tell? I don't even know what we've got.

Peter

Count them.

Eleanor

That's a good idea. (begins counting) Twenty. Twenty-six. Thirty. Thirty-four. I can only make it thirty-four. I think there were thirty-five. Am I right?

Peter

I don't know. I didn't count them in the first place.

Eleanor

Neither did I.

Peter

Well, what's the use of counting then?

Eleanor

Well, it was your idea.

Peter

Damn!

Eleanor

Whatever shall we do?

Peter

We could call the police.

Eleanor

That's out of the question. Besides, we can't even say what's missing, because we don't know.

Peter

Yes, because you didn't count them as they came in.

Eleanor

I suppose you couldn't have counted them?

Peter

I was too busy greeting the guests.

Eleanor

Sampling the port.

Peter

Just like a woman, to blame her husband for her own mistake.

Eleanor

I shall scream.

(They walk up and down, and ignore each other.)

Peter

The mean pig hasn't even brought us a present. I'm hanged if he shall carry one off.

Eleanor

I have it.

Peter

You remembered how many gifts we received?

Eleanor

No.

Peter

Then, what?

Eleanor

He's going to...he's sure to take a bath.

Peter

What do you suggest? Hiding his clothes?

Eleanor

Don't be so dull. He's bound to leave his keys somewhere. You'll go through his luggage while he's bathing.

Peter

But, that's uncivilized.

Eleanor

It's the only thing to do. It's the only way to avoid a scandal.

Peter

I won't do it.

Eleanor

You must.

Peter

Would you have me rifle the luggage of a guest? Besides, it's against the law.

Eleanor (heroically)

I'll stand look-out!

Peter

I'll do it.

(They go out, talking about details as the lights dim. Pause. When the lights go back up, Peter and Lady Eleanor reenter furtively.)

Peter

The cunning brute. He took a cream jug, because there were so many. He thought it wouldn't be missed.

Eleanor

Put it back with the others.

(Peter places the jug with the other jugs. Enter Wilfred. Peter and Lady Eleanor jump like frightened cats. Wilfred has an air of outrage about him.)

Wilfred

Oh, here you are, Peter. I've been looking all over for you. Finally, it occurred to me, you said you would be standing guard here.

Peter (uneasily)

Looking for me, were you?

Eleanor

Whatever for, at this time of night?

Peter

I thought you must be asleep by now.

Wilfred

It's a good thing you were standing watch here. Something most unpleasant has happened.

Eleanor (with exquisitely feigned concern)

What is it?

Wilfred

There's a thief in the house. Good thing I warned you to stand guard over the gifts.

Peter

A thief in this house, ha, ha. Impossible.

Wilfred

I'm sure of it. Something's been taken from my portmanteau.

Eleanor (astonished)

Really?

Peter (to Eleanor, low)

What gall.

Wilfred

What say, Peter?

Peter

I said, I hope you didn't leave your luggage in the hall?

Wilfred

By no means. It was in my room. Must have happened while I was in the bath.

Peter

This is really dreadful.

Wilfred

Perhaps, we'd better call the police.

Eleanor (scared)

Oh, no.

Peter (to Eleanor)

Nerves of steel. He lies like a politician. What effrontery. Call the police against the owners of the property you've stolen.

Wilfred

I realize calling the police is unpleasant, especially at a festive occasion like this.

Eleanor (significantly)

Yes. All the guests would have to be investigated. I've sure Scotland Yard does quite thorough background checks.

Wilfred (unperturbed by this warning)

Very unpleasant for you, and particularly Diana. But, it's the right thing to do.

Peter

Perhaps there's a kleptomaniac in the house?

Eleanor

Yes, everyone's background would be investigated, even the complainant's.

Wilfred

It is rather a nasty business. But, I paid over two hundred pounds for it in Cairo.

Peter

Paid that much. Whatever is it, anyway?

Wilfred

A silver cream jug, very like the seven others you have. I bought it for Diana as a present from myself and my mother.

Eleanor

A silver cream jug?

Peter

What a coincidence.

Wilfred

Exactly. It's slightly different, Arabic markings. But, after seeing all those duplicates, I'd have felt like a fool giving it to you, so I decided to exchange it in the morning.

Peter (dryly)

Exceedingly kind of you.

Wilfred

Now, it's gone. (pause) Mother will be most upset.

Eleanor

Did you say your mother?

Wilfred

Yes, of course.

Peter

I thought your mother had been dead for some time?

Wilfred

Oh, no. Lady Constance is quite well, thank you. No, no, it's Lady Margaret who is dead. You know, the Snatcher's mother.

Eleanor and Peter

The Snatcher!

Wilfred

I say, he's not here, is he? That would explain a lot.

Peter

Oh, no. We'd never invite him. And, he would never come.

Wilfred

I should hope not. Even all that money he's inherited shouldn't buy him entrance in a respectable home like this. Still, if he were here, that would explain everything.

Peter (weakly)

So it would. (to Eleanor) It's Wilfred the Attaché. I remember him now.

Eleanor

It would be much better to have the Snatcher here, than to think there are thieves in the house.

Wilfred

That's a way of looking at it. I haven't seen the Snatcher in many years, poor devil. It must be very embarrassing to be a kleptomaniac.

Peter

Embarrassing for his hosts, too.

Eleanor

One doesn't quite know what to do in such situations.

Wilfred

But, think of the fear of being caught. I mean, for a person of good family, who is otherwise respectable.

Peter (morosely)

Agonizing...absolutely agonizing.

Eleanor (nervously)

Just terrible.

Wilfred

Dr. Freud says they get sexual gratification from it. Makes them randy.

Peter (who is having trouble standing in one place)

Seems like something one could do without.

Wilfred

We've really go to do something abut the present incident. No use standing around talking. Whoever the wretch is, he must be brought to justice.

Peter (devastated)

Wretch is not quite the word I would use.

Wilfred

Well, what else can you call him, and remain without the limits of decorum? Swine, perhaps.

Eleanor

Perhaps, someone who simply made a mistake.

Wilfred

A mistake! Don't be so charitable, Lady Eleanor. A mistake like that will put him in gaol for ten years.

Peter (aghast)

Ten years!

Wilfred

That's the most you can expect these days from the bleeding hearts on the bench. Something should be done about the penal system in this country. Puts criminals right back on the street.

Eleanor

But, what if it were someone we knew?

Wilfred

What of it? He's a swine, that's all. I tell you, I mean to prosecute.

Peter and Eleanor

Prosecute!

Wilfred

Well, certainly. We cannot leave people like that running around. Menace to society, and all that.

(During this scene Peter and Lady Eleanor have tried to put themselves between Wilfred and the cream jugs.)

Eleanor

But, perhaps, if the jug were returned, surely you would...?

Wilfred

Nonsense. I'm a man of principle. It's not the cost of the jug that's important. I waste as much in a week gambling. It's the idea of its being stolen.

Peter (with desperation)

Before we go too far, we should establish that you haven't lost or misplaced it.

Wilfred

Lost it? I should think not. I haven't even taken it from my luggage. It was when I was looking for my pajamas after taking my bath that I discovered it was missing.

Eleanor

Perhaps, in all the excitement...?

Wilfred

Dear lady Eleanor, I know how you like to make excuses to avoid unpleasantness. But the fact will not go away, that there's a thief in the house.

Eleanor

Perhaps, if we looked around.

Wilfred

Where would one look?

Eleanor (losing her head completely)

Here, perhaps.

Wilfred

Why here? A thief would hide it here.

Eleanor

You never know. Hiding something in plain sight is supposed to be ever so clever. (counting the jugs) Why, there are eight jugs here. I only remember seven. (wildly) You must have brought it here yourself before you went to your bath.

(Wilfred stares open-mouthed at Lady Eleanor.)

Peter (with desperate heartiness)

One's mind often plays one little tricks like that. Why, only the other day I went to town to pay a bill, only to find I had paid it the day before. Clean forgot.

Wilfred (grimly)

My memory is better than that, Cousin Peter. (looking at the jugs and holding one up) But, this is certainly the jug I bought for you.

(Wilfred has evidently concluded in his own mind that he is in the presence of the thief or thieves, but hasn't quite made up his mind what to do. Lady Eleanor perceives his state of mind and prepares to take resolute action to avert a disaster. She collapses in a semi-faint.)

Eleanor

Peter, get my smelling salts, dear. I think they're in my dressing room.

Peter (rushing out with ill-concealed gratification at so happy a delivery)

At once, my dear! At once. (aside) Never so glad to get out of a room in my life.

Eleanor (rising as soon as Peter leaves)

Thank God, he's gone. Now, I can explain.

Wilfred

Are you all right, Lady Eleanor? Good. As for explaining, I'm sure I've never seen anything less in need of explanation in my life. It's cruelly obvious what has happened. I have an unpleasant duty to do, that's all.

Eleanor

Surly a diplomat like you will know how to treat this as if it hadn't happened? Peter's little weakness; it runs in the family.

Wilfred (shocked)

Good Lord! Do you mean to say he's a kleptomaniac like Cousin Snatcher?

Eleanor (mildly)

Not exactly like the Snatcher. He would never touch anything he found lying about. But he can't resist raiding things that are locked up.

Wilfred

You must have a terrible time, Lady Eleanor. You have all my sympathy.

Eleanor (the martyred wife)

Thank you for your support, Wilfred. One needs someone who understands.

Wilfred

Brave little woman.

Eleanor (tragically)

He must have pounced on your luggage the moment you went to your bath. (with tears in her eyes) Of course, he had no motive in taking your cream jug. We have seven already. Not that we don't value your gift. Shhh! He's coming.

Wilfred (heroically)

I quite understand. Count on me.

Peter

Here are your salts, darling. (holding them out to her)

Eleanor

Bring it here. (whispering to him) It's all right. I've explained everything to him. Don't say any more about it.

Peter (jubilant and proud)

Heroic woman. I don't know how you did it. I couldn't.

Eleanor (low to Peter)

Be glad you have a wife, like me. Finesse. (aloud) Help me up. I need to rest. Please excuse us.

Wilfred

Certainly, Lady Eleanor. (to himself) Poor martyr.

(Lady Eleanor goes out, supported by Peter. Then Wilfred goes out. The lights dim. When the lights go up again, it is the next morning. Sun shines through the windows. Wilfred enters, with his luggage, ready to leave.)

Wilfred

Well, I must say, it's been a strange night. Who would have thought that Cousin Peter shared the Snatcher's proclivities? (he looks at the gifts) At least I've warned the other guests.

(The servant enters, laughing.)

Servant (tittering)

I've never seen anything like it. All the guests are carrying their luggage to the bathroom with them. Sometimes two or three pieces.

Wilfred

It certainly is unusual. But, perhaps, it's a necessary precaution (low) in this house.

(The servant leaves.)

Wilfred (still looking at the gifts)

A shame that such a weakness should run in so respectable a family. (examining the silver dish) This will go perfectly with the tea service I obtained from the Thai embassy. (with a practices sweep of his hand, the dish vanishes into his suitcase) Well, I'd better be going before Peter starts rummaging through my things again.

(Wilfred leaves. The curtain starts to fall, hesitates, then rises again. Lady Eleanor and Peter enter.)

Peter

Well, I, for one, am glad that is over.

Eleanor

It was most trying. It's a good thing I have a certain social sense. It would have killed most women, making a mistake like that.

Peter

In the unwritten annals of domestic heroism, you have certainly earned a prominent place.

Eleanor

So silly to think that the Attaché was the Snatcher.

(Enter a servant with a salver. The servant presents it to Peter, who takes a card.)

Peter

Ridiculous of us to get so upset, and make such an error.

Eleanor

The Snatcher would never show up.

(Peter looks at the card and, without saying a word, weakly hands it to his wife.)

Eleanor

Oh, no, it can't be.

Peter (groaning)

It is. The Snatcher. He's come.

(Lady Eleanor collapses. Peter is too weak to go for the smelling salts himself, and the servant runs out, shrieking. This time the curtain falls.)

CURTAIN

VIOLENT ATTACHMENTS
OR, A PEEP INTO THE EIGHTEENTH CENTURY: A SHORT COMEDY INSPIRED BY AN ANONYMOUS EIGHTEENTH-CENTURY NOVEL

CAST OF CHARACTERS

LADY EASY

JOHN, her footman

LADY PAM

LORD FAWN, a fortune-hunting nobleman

COUNT OF MONTE VERDE, a pretended Count

ACT I
SCENE 1

A roadway that gives on a park.

Enter Lady Easy and her coachman, John. Lady Easy is very distraught.

Lady Easy

Oh John, John, I shall expire!

John

Yes, your ladyship.

Lady Easy

Can the fool do nothing but repeat what I say? Well, this confirms me in the fatality of dreams. But, we must submit to fate. Well, don't just stand there like a bumpkin. See if you can rectify what's amiss, John.

John

The coach can be fixed, but it will be impossible to set things to right in less than three hours, ma'am.

Lady Easy

Oh, but do try to hurry. I am on the most important journey of my life, John, and this horrible accident may prevent me from meeting my fate in Hertford, John. Think of that, John.

John

Very somber, your ladyship, very somber.

Lady Easy

But I must patiently submit to my fate. I am deservedly punished, for I might have avoided this ghastly accident by attending to what my dream predicted.

(declaiming) Heaven made us agents free to good or ill,

And forced it not, though He foresaw it all.

Freedom was first bestowed on human race,

And prescience only held the second place,

If He could make such agents wholly free,

I'll not dispute—

John

Hem, if it please your ladyship, I couldn't help it, 'pon honor, madam, I couldn't, and as for disputing with your ladyship, I hope—

Lady Easy

You misapprehend me, John, it was not with you that I was disputing—

John (looking around in bewilderment)

As you please, my lady, but—

Lady Easy (irritated)

I was quoting Dryden.

John

Yes, your ladyship. (after a pregnant pause) I think, your ladyship, we are in luck—we cannot be far from Lady Pam's.

Lady Easy (back to her quoting)

I'll write whatever time shall bring to pass

With pens of adamant on plates of brass.

John

M'lady?

Lady Easy (noticing him)

Eh? What would you have, John?

John

We cannot be far from Lady Pam's.

Lady Easy

But, we are totally unacquainted, John. Still, I have longed to meet her—I've been told we resemble each other very much. And she's a distant relation, or something, so, perhaps, it would not be too much of an imposition, if— Yet, I would not deviate one iota from the strict rules of polite fashion, despite my distress—so, I think it better—

(Enter Lord Fawn.)

Lord Fawn

Good afternoon, your ladyship. (bowing) Perhaps I may be of some assistance. I saw the condition of your coach. As mine is in good repair, may I offer to accompany you wherever you like?

Lady Easy

You are far too gracious. If you could give me a lift to Lady Pam's, which is not too far from here, I should be eternally grateful.

Lord Fawn

Lady Pam? Why, we are on the edge of her estate. Indeed, I was going thither myself, to pay her my respects, as I am an ardent admirer of hers, though she treats me despicably— If I am not mistaken, that is she approaching—

Lady Easy

What a stroke of luck.

Lord Fawn

Wonderful, madam. Here comes the dear creature now.

Lady Easy

Why, you must be Lord Fawn?

Lord Fawn

I confess it, madam. And, by your looks—your resemblance to Lady, Pam—you must be Lady Easy.

Lady Easy

You've hit it.

(Enter Lady Pam. She has a dog and a monkey with her.)

Pam, Lord Fawn, your servant.

Lord Fawn (simpering)

Lady Pam, may I present someone most desirous of making your acquaintance—the adorable Lady Easy.

(Lady Pam and Lady Easy bow to each other, and then hurl themselves into a furious embrace.)

Pam

My dear, I am superlatively happy in this favor. You'll pardon me, my lord, but Lady Easy's goodness in this visit is so immense, that I positively believe I shall not be able to speak a syllable for a month.

Lady Easy

Dear Lady Pam, this happiness is entirely on my side; such a celestial accident—if an accident of the same kind was always productive of such a felicity, I should entreat my stars to permit my coach to break down every day of my life.

Lord Fawn

But, ladies—

Lady Easy

Excuse me, my lord, I must entreat you to grant me permission to intrude so far on your lordship's patience as not to lay myself under the odium of impoliteness by a remissness in returning a suitable thanks to dear Lady Pam. But I am in such a flutter that I positively conceive that I labor under the same predicament as your ladyship, for I really do not believe I shall be able to utter a single sentence till the sun has made another revolution; but beg your ladyship's fertile imagination will form the finest turned sentence that ever fancy wore—and—oh, I am speechless—

Lord Fawn

But, ladies—

Pam

My lord, your pardon, I would wait upon your lordship immediately, but dear Lady Easy is so ravishingly kind, so immensely polite, so enchantingly condescending, so, so, so— Excuse me, my lord, I really have not the power of speech. (aside to Lord Fawn) I don't like her very much—

Lord Fawn

Dear ladies, if I might—

Pam

In good time, my lord, but politeness in excess is a debt which demands instantaneous payment, and I am very punctual in keeping up my credit in decorum, therefore, dear Lady Easy— bless me, how infertile my tongue is today—I have not a thought worthy of such excellence, nor an expression to convey my sense of your goodness. I'm stupid, absolutely dumb.

Lord Fawn (bowing)

Ladies, I humbly take my leave. I'll look to the coach. Come, John.

John

Yes, your lordship.

Lady Easy (curtly to Lord Fawn)

My lord, your most obedient— (effusively to Lady Pam) Dear Lady Pam, you've got a most enchanting monkey.

(brusquely to Lord Fawn) I humbly thank your lordship for— (about to expire, to Lady Pam) What's your monkey's name, my dear? (to Lord Fawn)—all your lordship's unparalleled favors. (turning her back on him to look at Lady Pam)

Pam

His name's Jacko, my dear. (indifferently) Adieu, my lord. (to Lady Easy) He's a diverting creature. (to Lord Fawn) I hope your lordship will let me see you again very speedily. (to Lady Easy and the monkey) Poor Jacko, poor Jacky, Jacky.

Lord Fawn

I'll do myself the pleasure of waiting upon your ladyship very soon. In the meantime, ladies, I kiss your hands.

(bowing and leaving) (aside) I've never been so insulted in my life.

(Exit Lord Fawn and John.)

Lady Easy

My lord, what a silly man. Indeed, your monkey is so ravishingly pretty, I could kiss him. But, pray, what's that lord?

Pam

A suitor of mine, my dear.

Lady Easy

You couldn't intend to marry a man so lacking in ton?

Pam

Heavens, no, I'd rather marry Jacko.

Lady Easy

Indeed, I prefer him myself. But, my dear, are you fond of poetry?

Pam

I'm fond of painting, my dear.

Lady Easy

It's all the same—they both delineate the affections of the soul. Celestial! So you love painting!

Pam

Oh, immensely!

Lady Easy

My dear Lady Pam, how happy we shall be in the congeniality of our ideas. Sir Francis once wrote to me that "I had no occasion to speak, for my eyes glanced my meaning." He even said I could "speak a look." But we were not destined for each other; I was cruel, extremely cruel; were you ever cruel, my dear?

Pam

My dear Lady Easy, can you entertain so mean a thought of my education as to think me capable of being otherwise? No, my dear, I delight in cruelty. It's the very food of my soul. Did you know I was very near losing my life once, attempting to mortify Miss Manly?

Lady Easy

How, my dear?

Pam

I'll tell you, my dear. Miss Manly was fond of hunting and had a white riding habit in which she was greatly admired. I had a much more elegant habit and was destined to eclipse her had not my horse thrown me. The wretch enjoyed my fall with the greatest satisfaction. But it was the vexation that nearly put an end to my life. But, thanks to youth and pride, I recovered and am, if possible, more cruel than ever.

(Enter John.)

John

We've set matters right at last, ma'am.

Lady Easy

I'll tell you what I've been thinking, John. As the accident was poetical—you for the future shall be called Phaeton.

John

Whatever your ladyship pleases.

Lady Easy

John, could you fancy the horses had fiery manes?

John,

Yes, if I saw them on fire.

Pam

Pshaw, the fellow's stupid.

Lady Easy (angrily)

Go to the coach and wait for orders.

John

Yes, ma'am. (exit)

Lady Easy

I think, Lady Pam, I was not misinformed, we are really very much alike; indeed, you have a trifling advantage over me with respect to beauty. (she takes out a mirror and looks at herself with great satisfaction, arranging a patch and a curl)

Pam

Dear Lady Easy, do not sacrifice your merit to your politeness—nor give another that which is so justly your own due. (primping) I am tolerable. But it was given to you, my dear, to be irresistible.

Lady Easy

Excuse me, my dear, you have the power to make your lovers slide.

Pam

Slide! Slide! (offended) You mean they slip away?

Lady Easy

Oh, no.

Beauty like ice our footsteps does betray,

Who can tread sure on the smooth slippery way.

Pam (mollified)

Ha, ha, ha. Oh, in that sense.

Lady Easy

You've got a pretty dog there, my dear.

Pam

Yes, my dear. Beauties are universally allowed him. He's been more caressed and courted by my lovers than even a statesman's pimp.

Lady Easy

He's an engaging creature.

Pam

Oh, he really has some sentiment.

Lady Easy

Indeed!

Pam

I'll assure you, some of his notions are very delicate. Why, he quite stopped Lord Moral, who passes for a wit, but who in reality is no better than a fool, from arguing with his usual impertinence that one half of the paintings bought for originals are only vile copies. My dear Guido began to yelp and bark in such a manner that he absolutely stopped my gentleman's insolent volubility—which together with my contemptuous attitude obliged him to retire in confusion.

Lady Easy

Sensible creature! You surely have a great value for him.

Pam

Oh! My love for him is inconceivable. He's the dearest, sweetest, loveliest little puppy. (she squeezes him and the dog yelps)

Lady Easy

But, what is that strange ribbon?

Pam

Oh, my dear, Guido's a knight. It is but a short time since I had him installed with great pomp in our large hall—oh, you must see our large hall, you'll die—and let me tell you, he bore his investiture with becoming decency.

Lady Easy

Pray, of what order is he knight?

Pam

Oh, my dear, the order of the painted gallery. But, would you like to hear his ancestry?

Lady Easy

My dear, you will oblige me infinitely.

Pam

Guido is descended from a family as ancient and renowned as any the four-footed race can boast of. He is a direct descendant of Towzer, a large bull dog belonging to Cardinal Wolsey when he was only a butcher. You smile, my dear. Perhaps you think it impossible for a butcher to become a minister of state?

Lady Easy

Excuse me, Lady Pam. I had no such thought, I assure you. Indeed, I have observed some ministers of state have turned butchers of late years.

Pam

To proceed. Towzer fell passionately in love with Miss Sleek, a bitch belonging to Henry the Eighth.

Lady Easy

He had so many bitches.

Pam

Their nuptials—for they were regularly married—were productive of a fine puppy named Sly. From Sly a train of statesmen regularly succeeded until the days of Oliver Cromwell. One of Sly's successors named Scarem belonged to Cromwell himself, and barked so loudly in the cause of liberty that any person who dared even mutter a syllable in favor of prerogative in his presence was sure to lose a piece of his leg.

Lady Easy

Wonderful.

Pam

And more wonderful, Scarem begot Supple, who gave himself up to the intrigues of court, and it is from one of Supple's private amours that my dear Guido is descended. He's the sweetest and best-tempered puppy existing.

(squeezing him) Yeowww!!! He bit me!

(Lady Pam faints.)

Lady Easy (thundering)

John! John! John! Oh, where is the fool?

(Enter John hurriedly.)

Lady Easy

Where have you been, John, all this time?

John

Nowhere, my lady.

Lady Easy

You must prepare a horse with all possible speed.

John (leaving)

Yes, your ladyship.

Lady Easy

Why, the fellow's stupid. Would you go without your message?

You must be as expeditious as possible. Hurry!

John (leaving)

Yes, your ladyship.

Lady Easy

Wait! You see poor Lady Pam is almost expiring. Let me see, what was I going to say? Oh, yes, be as quick as possible.

John

Yes, your ladyship. I will go immediately.

Lady Easy

Where is the fool hurrying? Stay and take your message with you. I did not tell you what to go for, did I?

John

No, your ladyship.

Lady Easy

No? Then, where would the simpleton be running? You must saddle a horse, I tell you—and when that is done—mount it, do you hear me?

John

Yes, your ladyship.

Lady Easy

Then, don't stand kicking your legs about and biting the corner of your hat in that manner, but mind what I say to you; when you have mounted the horse—for you must make an expedition—for the lady is positively dying—and don't founder in the mud.

John

No, your ladyship. There is no danger of that. The roads are not muddy.

Lady Easy

Incorrigible animal, be silent! The roads are not muddy? What incorrigible and ridiculous ideas the fool has. The roads are always muddy. But mind, you must make all the haste you can to London, and do you mind me.

John (frustrated)

Yes, your ladyship.

Lady Easy

A fiddlestick cannot hold your tongue. Take notice of what I say. When you get to London, you must tell Clytemnestra—

John

I don't know any such gentleman, your ladyship.

Lady Easy

Egregious blockhead, be silent. "I don't know any such

gentleman." Truly. Why, stupidity itself realized it's no gentleman, but my waiting maid, Molly, under her poetic name. You must tell her to look in Cyclops's eyes and send me a small thumb vial which she'll find there—for nothing else will be efficacious toward the recovery of this lady.

John

Yes, ma'am. Who is Cyclops?

Lady Easy

Who is Cyclops? Fool! Cyclops is my dressing table.

John

To be sure, ma'am.

(Exit John.)

Pam (groaning)

Ohh!

Lady Easy

Will you live, dear Lady Pam?

Pam (getting up with assistance)

Yes, I believe so. Yes, I will live.

Lady Easy (clapping her hands and jumping up and down)

How wonderful! How celestial! Lady Pam will live.

Pam (fanning herself)

I think I am myself, again. But, I am so impolite. I've totally forgotten to ask you the reason for your journey, and whither you are bent.

Lady Easy

You must know, my dear, that I'm a very odd creature, immensely whimsical. (confidentially) I love dearly to pry into futurity.

Pam

Aren't you scared?

Lady Easy

I'm absolutely frightened to death of almost everything I discover. Terrible!

Pam

Terrible.

Lady Easy

If I could make things happen according to my wish I should be the happiest creature existing; but when I want a thing to happen one way, I find a prediction informing me it shall happen another. Which you know, my dear, is enough to give one the spleen.

Pam

When I have a great inclination to do what I should not, I never once consult the stars, for fear they should forbid me.

Lady Easy

What a charming thing it would be if one could always enjoy one's wishes, and follow one's inclinations and yet never suffer for it.

Pam

My dear, it is totally impossible for a pretty woman to do wrong. A woman has only to fancy she is right in order to be so. All the men allow it, and they are held to be very wise.

Lady Easy

My dear, I shall adopt your maxims. They seem so replete with conveniences.

Since angels feel, whose strength was more than mine,

T'would show more grace, my frailty to confine—

Well, to get back to my journey, one day I found a paper in Cyclops's eyes. Cyclops, my dear, is my name for my bureau.

Pam

Very poetic.

Lady Easy

I think so, too. We are so like-minded. Well, the paper must have got there miraculously, for I always keep it locked and my woman, to whom I have given the poetical name Clytemnestra—

Pam

Divine inspiration—

Lady Easy

—swore that she knew nothing of it.

Pam

What a mystery! What did it say?

Lady Easy

It said, "Celinda"—that's my poetical name—"will be unfortunate in her nuptials, unless she married Torrismond—the only man on earth destined to make her happy. He will be, tomorrow, in the bulwark of the head of a beast framed for swiftness between the two horns."

Pam

This is immense.

Lady Easy

Now, my dear, this prophecy being to me totally unintelligible rendered me almost distracted. I read it backwards and forwards, and every way, but I could make nothing of it. Then, John told me he had a relation who was a fortune teller. My coachman is of gypsy stock. Had I not gone to see him, I should never have resolved the matter.

Pam

Then, he was able to explain it?

Lady Easy

Easily. The place signified in the prophecy is the castle of Hertford. The Saxon word from which Hertford derives its name means "hart" or hare, a beast famed for its swiftness. The bulwark of the head is the castle, because the town is shaped like a capital Y. The name Torrismond is probably the adopted or poetical name of the person meant.

Pam

So easily explained. This fellow must be a prodigious fortune teller.

Lady Easy

Oh, my dear, he is the best I ever met. For, though he had told my fortune twenty times over, he never told me the same thing twice. Anyway, I immediately ordered my coach and was posting thither when I met this accident which has been the cause of procuring me your agreeable company.

Pam

And, if you should meet the person named in the prophecy, would you marry him, my dear?

Lady Easy

Oh, yes—we must submit to fate, you know, Lady Pam. But as I shall be sure of him—for he can no more act against the will of his stars than myself—I shall use him immoderately ill. For I think it the most delightful amusement to use a lover that dotes upon one to distraction—like a dog. Believe me, dear Lady Pam, I've occasioned the death of four hopeful young men already.

Pam

How unfortunate I have been to have had only one lover die upon my account. Indeed, his death gave me a great deal of uneasiness, for he hanged himself. If he had been killed in a duel or shot himself through the head, I should not have cared. But to have a lover hang himself, like a common criminal, frets one because it's vulgar. He was not thinking of ME when he did that! But, how did yours die?

Lady Easy

Why, I played off two of them with so much spirit against each other that, mad with jealousy, they fought a duel and both died of their wounds. But not before the most tender expressions of love were sent me from their death beds. A third fairly fretted to death, and the other shot himself through the head after I vexed him by sleeping with his brother. (sighing) If I could but kill a dozen, I should be supremely happy.

Pam

My dear, you are already on the road to happiness. I envy your triumphs. Suppose, my dear, we profess a violent attachment to each other?

Lady Easy

That will render my life a continual scene of ecstasy, my dear. I'm fond to excess of violent attachments. Let us be eternal and unchangeable friends from this moment. One fate, one fame, one faith, shall both attend my life's companion, and my bosom friend.

(They embrace.)

Pam

We shall share everything.

Lady Easy

Tastes.

Pam

Clothes.

Lady Easy

Books.

Pam

Paintings.

Lady Easy

Lovers.

Pam

Ecstasy.

Lady Easy

Look, my dear, here comes that odious Lord Fawn.

Pam

Faugh, I can't stand him. Now, my dear Lady Easy, as you were pleased to doubt my disposition to cruelty—though I do dote upon his lordship—you shall see me treat him in as cavalier a manner as any woman in the British Dominions—nay, the entire continent—if you will just hide behind that bush and listen.

(Lady Easy smiles and steps behind a tree. Lord Fawn enters.)

Lord Fawn

Dear Lady Pam—

Pam

Dear Lord Fawn.

Lord Fawn

When I first saw you, madam, you are aware I did not court you after the vulgar mode of the uneducated by proposing marriage. No, I thought you handsome enough to be a mistress and offered you a genteel settlement to surrender upon honorable terms, for as I hope to be cuckolded by a Prince of the Blood, I did not imagine you were so well off. But, since I find you are not under necessity of playing a fair game, and treating upon honorable terms, I must edge in and hang out the matrimonial flag.

Pam

My lord, you are extremely well-bred, and I should certainly have accepted your charming offer, but I feared you would have tyrannized over me. But, you know, if we marry, it is your place to submit.

Lord Fawn

Doubtless. A woman's powers, like her charms, should be

unbounded.

Pam

And yet, some men are such brutes that they use their mistresses like slaves and treat their wives in such an egregious manner that some silly people would be inclined to think it was the duty of a wife to be obedient.

Lord Fawn

They must be silly people indeed who could think such a thing. However, you'll find me a very obedient husband.

Pam

Well, my lord, you know a certain wit said:

—Horses and asses, we're allowed to try

And sound suspected vessels ere we buy,

Women a random choice, untried we take,

We dream in courtship, and in wedlock wake,

Then, not till then, the veil's removed, and the woman glares in open day.

Thus, if all these sarcastical strokes are true, my lord, I hope we have the same right to try your sex beforehand.

Lord Fawn (leering and trying to kiss her)

By all means, dear madam.

Pam (breaking away)

Then, I'll exact proof of your obedience. Have you ever heard of Sebastiano Conco?

Lord Fawn

No, madam, I cannot say I have, or at least my memory betrays me.

Pam

Dear me, why, he was born at Gaella in the year 1676, and died in 1764.

Lord Fawn

Very possible, madam, but I cannot say I recollect anything of the affair.

Pam

Well, that's amazing. He was a celebrated painter.

Lord Fawn

Indeed. I can't deny it, madam.

Pam

He studied under Luca Giordano. Now, you must know that a certain painter in the city of Rome has a certain painting of Sebastiano's. The subject is a silly boy killing a butterfly. Now, as I shall never be happy until I am possessed of that inimitable composition, I must insist that, ere Hymen unite us, you make a journey to Rome, discover the painter, and purchase the piece at whatever price is affixed to it.

Lord Fawn

Consider, dear Lady Pam, what cruelty it will be to banish me so long from your delightful presence. Let us first be joined in matrimony, and. then, we can go in search of this—masterpiece—together.

Pam

Clever fox. Nay, my lord. Stand to your promise, either drop the negotiation, or stand to the conditions prescribed. Besides, the journey will improve your taste infinitely, which, I assure you, will not be your least recommendation in my favor.

Lord Fawn

Damnation! I shall set off in the morning, Lady Pam.

Pam

You may kiss my hand before you go.

Lord Fawn

Infinite thanks, dear lady. (kissing her hand, he bows and leaves) Curses! Now, how shall I avoid this nuisance?

Pam

Well, how did you like that little farce, my dear?

Lady Easy

Infinitely. It will teach him how to be a devoted husband.

Pam

You are perfectly right, my dear. The creatures should be taught their duty.

Lady Easy

Certainly, my dear. We were born for prerogative and pleasure only—two principles the female sex obey, the love of pleasure and the love of sway. But, do you really love this male thing, my dear?

Pam

Oh, yes. I love him because all my friends have spoken against him, and done all in their power to prevent his visits. But, I'll do what I please, even if I suffer for it. Obstinacy is a delicious thing for a woman of spirit. The only way to make me do a thing is to persuade me not to do it.

Lady Easy

That, my dear, is a piece of finesse by which I was very near suffering. My uncle knew my disposition well, and artfully persuaded me not to marry a man I never intended to have. I was on the point of marrying the hideous creature when, by luck, I discovered my uncle's treachery and avoided the impending ruin.

Pam

What a dreadful escape.

Lady Easy (screaming)

Aiee!!!

Pam

What ails you, my dear?

Lady Easy

I shall miss my meeting with Torrismond. My life is ruined.

Pam

But, your coach is repaired, is it not?

Lady Easy

But when you fainted, I had John saddle a horse and ride to London to get you a cordial. He won't be back for hours. Oh, my unlucky stars!

Pam

But, you must use my coach, my dear.

Lady Easy

You are the most considerate creature.

Pam

Come, we'll see to it immediately.

(Pam and Lady Easy exit. A moment later, John enters furtively from the opposite direction.)

John

Saddle a horse and go to London, indeed! Tell Clytemnestra to look in Cyclops's eye—my black arse! So, what must I tell her? I have it—the horse fell in the mud and refused to go further. She'll call me stupid and say she told me so. And that will be the end of that. The woman's a fool. Clytemnestra, or Molly, as she is known to the rest of mankind, has more sense than my lady, and she can't read or write.

'Tis strange that man will always quit

The very thing for which he's fit.

His Grace is in 'Change—alley great,

While barbers regulate the State.

And some are so extremely wise,

They'd rule the rulers of the skies,

Though mortals seize the immortal rod,

And criticize the works of God,

A certain self-sufficient spark.

Parading o'er a rural park,

Viewed nature's charms with scornful eye,

And could in each a defect espy.

Puffed with importance, "Had," said he,

"The Universe been made by me,

Without a fault this world had rose,

No crimes, no murders, frauds, or woes,

The sun had given continual light.

But, now all things confused are found,

The noble pumpkin on the ground,

Mean acorns on that lofty tree,

These blunders had been changed by me.

Pumpkins to oaks had owed their birth,

And acorns spread from humble earth,"

He said, and crept beneath the shade,

To slumber on the verdant glade.

The branches shook as winds arose,

An acorn fell and hit his nose.

Conceited fool! Had things been made

According to the schemes you've laid,

Then, had your stupid head been crushed,

Your whim's destroyed and nonsense hushed.

Well, if all goes well, my silly mistress is riding for a fall in Hertford. Torrismond, ha, ha, ha.

Lord Fawn (entering furtively)

Hsstt!

John (startled)

Who's that?

Lord Fawn

Honest John, it's me, Lord Fawn.

John

You quite frightened me, sir.

Lord Fawn

My apologies. I need your help, John.

John

If I can, your lordship.

Lord Fawn

My mistress, Lady Pam, has sent me on the most silly wild goose chase that ever fair lady appointed a faithful, gullible knight. And I am determined to be revenged on her.

John

Yes, your lordship.

Lord Fawn

And, moreover, I suspect your mistress instigated Lady Pam to do it.

John

Not altogether unlikely, my lord. My mistress is terribly malicious.

Lord Fawn

Lady Pam insists I am to go to Rome to find a picture by Sebastiano Conco and bring it to her. Now, is that not absurd?

John

Rome is a long way off, sir.

Lord Fawn

Quite. But you must help me.

John,

But, how am I do to that, sir?

Lord Fawn

If I am not much mistaken in physiognomy, you, sir, are unmistakably an Italian?

John

Sir, I am a true-born Englishman. By the Holy Virgin, I—

Lord Fawn

By the Holy Virgin, I have you—no Englishman would swear so. You are no John, you are a Giovanni, or I lose my wager.

John

Please, sir, do not tell my mistress. She would turn me out, sure. She hates Italians.

Lord Fawn

Piano, piano, good Giovanni. I mean you no harm. Indeed, I will pay you well for assisting me.

John (excitedly)

Grazie, grazie. But, how am I to help you?

Lord Fawn

You must not think me such a fool as to contemplate going to Italy to find this silly painting. Now, I never knew an Italian, but he had some relative who could sing or paint. Have you such a relative, Giovanni?

John

Certo, certo, my brother Carlo.

Lord Fawn

Good, good. And could he paint a Sebastiano?

John (regaining his composure)

Certainly, my lord. He could paint a Michelangelo or a da Vinci. He's a wonderful forger.

Lord Fawn

Friend of my youth—let us become better acquainted. Now, what I need is a Sebastiano—the subject: a boy killing a butterfly.

(They exit in deep conversation)

BLACKOUT

ACT I
SCENE 2

When the lights go up, Lady Easy and Lady Pam enter, hugging each other.

Lady Easy

Dear, Auristella, for that is the poetical name I have, after mature deliberation fixed upon you, congratulate me, sing twenty Io paeans for me; I have seen the dear, predestinated, angelic man. Oh—he's all that painting can express, or youthful poets fancy when they love.

Pam

Is he so adorable, my dear? But, who is he?

Lady Easy

Upon my reputation, you'll never guess. I never saw him before, nor you neither, I believe. He's an Italian Count on his travels. His family owns half of Italy, I believe.

Pam

This is simply immense.

Lady Easy

My dear, I'm rapt, I'm in Elysium. I'm as happy as a seraph—but I may yet be happier—enchanting thought.

Pam

But, proceed regularly, and tell me the beginning, middle, and the end of things, in order.

Lady Easy

After I went off in your coach, I arrived at Hertford. And sure enough, the town is in the form of a capital Y. The castle is right in the middle. Upon enquiry, I found the castle turned into a boarding school. The master—

Pam

—is Torrismond?

Lady Easy

Heavens no, my dear. The master is an old gentleman who has the gout, very bad. The schoolmaster received me while he was teaching and paid an equal attention to me and his scholars. (imitating him)

Madam, your servant.

The regimen of verbs may be divided into three classes.

Pray, madam, be seated.

The first class is that of verbs personal.

What may have procured the honor of your visit, madam?

You blockhead, keep your tongue silent and mind me!

Pam

Ha, ha, ha.

Lady Easy

My Torrismond at this moment entered, and was called to by name by one of the boys. He bowed to me. (sighing)

He makes a sweet bow—and has a more agreeable smile than any man in Europe. I shall be a happy creature, for I'm sure of him and, you know, the stars must be obeyed.

Pam

Oh, to be as lucky as you. How I envy you.

Lady Easy

He has in infinity of wit. My heart palpitated the whole time.

Pam

But, were you cruel?

Lady Easy

It will be time enough to be cruel after we're married. The inimitable creature has written poetry to me—and so soon. Ah, Italians are so wonderful. Suppose, my dear, upon Lord Fawn's return you marry him and we four will form a coterie of our own. I love coteries dearly. I wish there were a thousand in

England. I'd do nothing but travel round the country and visit them all.

Pam

But, how on earth did an Italian Count find himself in Hertford Castle?

Lady Easy

It's the most immense story: Torrismond came to fulfill a vow and a prophecy.

Pam

Amazing. Immense. Come to the house, my dear, you must tell me all. Absolutely all.

(Lady Easy and Lady Pam leave, still deeply engaged in conversation. After a moment, enter John and the Count from another direction.)

Count

Well, brother Giovanni, the train has happily taken, and I am in a fair way to blow up the outworks, and hope soon to be in possession of the town.

John

Did I not tell you it would take, Carlo? This English woman is a complete fool. Pazzo!

Count

She really is a very agreeable woman in person, and would be every way charming if she could contrive to lose her affectation. But, that's not necessary at present, or even desirable. It's not my business to fall in love.

John

Brother, if you should ever fall in love with that woman, I would cut your heart out.

Count

Hey, Giovanni, do you want her for yourself?

John (crossing himself)

Never! But ever since I joined her service, she has lorded it over me in such a way that I will never forgive her, and must be revenged upon her.

Count

If I am not mistaken, I shall have a considerable deal of trouble with this fantastical lady yet. But if I get her, matrimony will soothe all sores. It was a stroke of genius to insert that prophecy into her bureau.

John

Into Cyclops's eye.

Count

What?

John

She calls her bureau Cyclops because it has only one drawer.

Count

The woman's as superstitious as a village witch.

John

It was my idea, brother.

Count

Agreed. You are the genius of this little comedy, Giovanni.

John

When she has married you, I can't wait to mortify her by telling her she has married the brother of a coachman.

Count

Even if you tell her, she'll never believe it.

John

Trust me, I'll make her believe it. But, tell me again how you met. I must hear all the details.

Count

Simple enough. I awaited my lady at Hertford Castle, which as you know is a boarding school run by our uncle.

There I encountered an unexpected obstacle. The old dog

pretended to have what the devil himself would never have suspected him of assuming, a conscience. He undertook to prove that I was going contrary to the strictest rules of propriety. But, I had that about me, Jack, that was too much for him. I clapped ten pounds into his hands, and he sagaciously found that my conduct was exactly consonant to the rules of grammar and the syllogism of logic. Is not money wonderful, brother? I instructed the boys to call me Torrismond. After the lady had arrived, and been with the gentleme\n ten minutes, I entered the school as if accidentally. One of the boys called out—Torrismond. It struck her. She was scarlet up to the neck. The pretty creature was ingenuously engaged in telling a hundred and fifty lies to get a sight of my sweet person.

John

Ha, ha. And this great lady calls me stupid.

Count

And as you will have a finger in the pie, pray to what saint you please, for the success of your brother, Torrismond, Count of Monte Verde.

John

As I hope to cuckold you with my mistress.

Count

But, I insist you wait until we are married.

John

But, of course.

Count

You were always after any wench I had run to ground, Jack.

John

You prefer the chase, I excel at the repast. At spitting the game, as it were.

Count

Oh, never mind! You may do with her as she will let you—once we are married and I have her portion nicely in my hands. Adultery will make a fine excuse for divorce. She is much more ridiculous than I could have conceived. I shall hate her abominably—but it doesn't matter. You know that to hate a wife is fashionable.

John

And, for the wife to take the footman privately to bed is—if not fashionable, at least common. Am I with you, brother?

Count

Damnation!

John

But come, I had forgotten, you must paint a picture for Lord Fawn.

Count

I no longer paint; I am a count now, and counts do not paint.

John

Your share will be a hundred pounds.

Count

On the other hand, even a nobleman should not throw away money.

BLACKOUT

ACT II
SCENE 3

A few weeks later; Lady Easy's sitting room.

John and the Count are talking.

John

To be blasted in all our projects when they were about to take so fairly!

Count

Unquestionably, there is no justice in the universe. Who could have expected that she would fall a victim to the smallpox, the very day before our wedding. Could she but have waited till we were married, I should not have cared. I was summoned last night. I had hopes she wanted to die a married woman. However, I was too sanguine in my expectations. She nearly killed me with scraps of execrable verse in praise of resignation. She told me she was going to express her gratitude for my continued attachment to her person. My heart beat an alarm of joy.

John

Perhaps she will leave you a legacy.

Count

I fancied that, too. I whined a bit to put her in the temper to improve upon her intentions. I put my handkerchief to my eye and "wiped away the tear I did not shed."

John

Did she do it, did she?

Count

I was horribly taken in. She made me executor and sole copyright holder of her execrable, nonsensical, and happily unpublished poetic drivel.

John

Fool! Why didn't you—? She's growing worse and worse. If she doesn't recover, you must transfer your affection to Lady Pam. I fancy she had a mind to you.

Count

One will do as well as the other. They are both equally ridiculous.

John

If she lives, her face will be scarified.

Count

I'm glad on it. It will give me an opportunity to pretend my passion is more than skin deep.

John

I think I should be happy for you to change her for Lady Pam.

Count

The deuce take the smallpox. I wish she were dead or well.

John

Lady Pam is with her now. If you wait here, you may have a chance to speak with her. Lose no opportunity.

Count

Rely on me, brother.

John

I hear her. I will leave you to better opportunity.

(Exit John.)

Count (alone)

Florio, a coxcomb of distinguished note,

Proud of the glitter of a laced coat,

Thought all embellishments of mind were low,

And much beneath the notice of a beau.

Oh, at a ball, to bear the belle away,

To be the sovereign arbiter at tea (tay),

These were concerns of most prodigious weight,

Enough to sink a minister of state.

He'd tell a lady, like a useful friend,

How a boiled lapdog might complexions mend,

Or give the greatest brilliancy to sight,

What made hands the most delicate white.

Long Florio roved about from Miss to Miss,

But never tasted one substantial bliss.

No single woman had sufficient charms

To captivate him to her lovely arms.

He thought each hair upon his head a dart,

And that each hair deserved a woman's heart.

Soft! She comes.

(Enter Lady Pam.)

Pam

Musing, poor forlorn man? Is the disorder of my friend a great affliction to your lordship?

Count

So much that I cannot explain it. Everything must affect a lover which endangers the life of a beloved mistress.

Pam

I dare say, my lord, you will be inconsolable for the loss of her beauty.

Count

Indeed, madam, you wrong me in your opinion. I should never pay adoration to beauty alone. There are other charms much more attractive to me. Alas, if beauty was my sole consideration, there are some who could inspire a much stronger passion than Lady Easy.

Pam (smiling)

Indeed, my lord. Why, I always took Lady Easy to be the handsomest woman in the kingdom.

Count

Then, your ladyship never viewed yourself in a proper light.

Pam

My lord, you grow rude. A compliment to me is an affront to my sick friend. Besides, you are insincere. You don't really think I am so handsome as Lady Easy.

Count

Your glass must convince you that I speak according to my conscience in giving you preference.

Pam

I have been reflecting on your pretended disregard for beauty. I find it not only unnatural, but impossible. I am certain you dissemble in compliment to my sick friend.

Count

'Pon honor, ma'am, I vow—

Pam

Stop! Do not vow. Lady Easy is shockingly scarified. The most advisable thing is to break off the whole affair.

Count

Madam! My honor—

Pam

No, don't protest. I know it is impossible for any man to fall in love with the mind unless he has a fancy to a beautiful face attached to it. Since I'm convinced you fell in love with my friend for her beauty, and that beauty is no more, it is a duty incumbent on the friendship I profess to her to prevent the match. For, if you had made her any promise, you high-minded man, your honor may prompt you to keep it. Yet, that coolness of behavior which necessarily follows distress, will make her forever miserable. Decidedly, she had better remain single, or at least, marry one who had never seen her during the meridian of her charms.

Count

Madam, I'm speechless, I—

Pam

Oh, it's unnecessary to speak. I know your mind. If I deprive you of what you once thought was a blessing, it is only proper I should make you some recompense.

Count

I don't know what to say.

Pam

You hoped to marry a beautiful woman. Because of me, you lose her. Command me, then—to the extent of my power.

Count

The only recompense you could make me, for depriving me of your friend, would be—to bless me with yourself.

Pam

That would be impossible! Well, I can refuse you nothing, poor thing.

Count

Allow me to retire to procure the license.

(The Count kisses Lady Pam's hand and exits. Pam, alone, fidgets about, then sits at the writing table.)

Pam (writing)

Dear Celinda, As your loss of beauty would undoubtedly have occasioned the loss of your betrothed's affections—that is, my dear, if you had married the count—I, out of the violence of my affection for you, and in the extremity of my attachment—have married him myself. That your delicate nerves might not suffer a shock by the coldness in my lord's behavior which the want of your charms would necessarily cause. Therefore, I hope you will consider this sacrifice on my part in its proper light—and believe I am, with as violent an attachment as ever, Your sincere friend, Auristella.

(Lady Pam leaves the letter on the writing desk and exits. After a moment, John enters. He reads the letter.)

John

Money has the power above

The stars and fate to manage love.

Those arrows, learned poets hold,

That never fail—are tipped with gold.

Now I think that Lord Fawn will be best advised to marry Lady Easy. But first, I must extract the money for the Sebastiano.

BLACKOUT

ACT II
SCENE 4

The same, some months later.

John and the Count. John is no longer dressed like a servant.

John

Well, I had much fancied myself to be Lady Easy's brother-in-law. But, as I am not related to Lord Fawn, that is impossible.

Count

Lady Pam resents you as much as Lady Easy would have, I'm sure.

John

No, I think Lady Easy would not have born it so well.

Count

Well, we are well come off. I am rich enough, so that I can pay my creditors.

John

Have you seen your wife lately?

Count

She hasn't spoken to me since she learned you were my brother.

John

I believe she has renewed her attachment to Lady Easy, I mean Lady Fawn.

Count

Yes. I believe that lady has no great use for her husband either.

John

Lord Fawn treats her with great politeness.

Count

She knew he was marrying her for her money; she has no right to complain.

John

I've heard she sighs for you on occasion.

Count

Sometimes, I wish—but, let that pass.

(Enter Lord Fawn.)

Fawn

My dear Count. (bowing)

Count

My dear Lord Fawn. (bowing lower)

Fawn

Well, my lord, how do you like matrimony?

Count

Oh! Excellently well. When all other amusements grow stale and insipid, I can always find an inexhaustible fund of entertainment in tormenting my wife. But, how does your lordship pass your time?

Fawn

Oh, in much the same manner. Lady Fawn and myself, every day, enjoy the sublime satisfaction of mortifying each other to the utmost extent of our considerable abilities.

Count

Damn it—my wife should have belonged to you, and yours to me.

Fawn

I must confess I fancied Lady Pam to the very utmost of the ton. I believe I could actually have fallen in love with her, if I had been given to that failing.

Count

And, I confess I had a small weakness for Lady Easy, before her bout of smallpox. Indeed, I don't care, but what—even though her beauty— Well, I say no more.

Fawn

Her beauty is much restored.

Count

Indeed?

Fawn

Unfortunately, her temper—

Count

That was never very good, yet—

Fawn

Since we have fallen out with our wives, they have fallen in again.

Count

Yes, they have renewed their violent attachment. (pause, musing) As we are in the zenith of fashion, my lord, suppose we strike a coup d'éclat.

Fawn

How, my lord?

Count

I'll tell you. We'll dice for 'em. Winner take both.

Fawn

In so doing, we shall play contrary to the practice of gamesters. For we shall both play with a desire to lose.

Count (producing dice)

Be that as it will, my lord, we shall be diverted. And, such a bet, you know, will be quite the thing. Will you throw, my lord?

Fawn

With the greatest pleasure. (throws)

Count

Ah—sixes. (throws) Snake eyes. Lady Pam is yours. (aside) How convenient are loaded dice.

Fawn

Dear, dear. I am so heartily sick of one wife, I fear two will be too much for me. Take your revenge, sir, please.

Count

But I will not dice for both.

Fawn

For mine only, then.

Count

Very well, but I had rather you keep 'em both. (throws)

Fawn

Sixes. (throws) Snake eyes. Lady Fawn is yours. (aside) Thank heavens I switched the dice.

John (clapping his hands)

Wonderful, my lords. This is in the very height of the ton.

Fawn

This is an affair of honor. The ladies must be informed immediately.

John

Allow me to have that privilege. I yearn to see Lady Fawn's face.

(Exit John. Enter Lady Fawn and Lady Pam.)

Pam

We overheard everything.

Lady Fawn

Nothing could be more agreeable.

Pam

This affair is polite in the highest degree.

Lady Fawn

This will render us a coterie and afford us the opportunity of enjoying variety.

Pam

Oh, I am so glad we have renewed our violent attachment to each other.

Lady Fawn

We are ready to comply immediately with the decrees of fate.

(Lady Fawn grasps the Count. Lady Pam pinches Lord Fawn.)

Lord Fawn (aghast)

Would I were so ready!

Lady Pam

Should you need assistance, we know where to procure the aid of a vigorous footman.

(Enter John.)

John

Did you call, my lady?

CURTAIN

John

The proverb holds:

That to be wise and love,

Is hardly granted to the gods above.

We ask your applause.

CURTAIN

ABOUT THE AUTHOR

Frank J. Morlock has written and translated many plays since retiring from the legal profession in 1992. His translations have also appeared on Project Gutenberg, the Alexandre Dumas Père web page, Literature in the Age of Napoléon, Infinite Artistries.com, and Munsey's (formerly Blackmask). In 2006 he received an award from the North American Jules Verne Society for his translations of Verne's plays. He lives and works in México.

www.ingramcontent.com/pod-product-compliance
Lightning Source LLC
LaVergne TN
LVHW041619070426
835507LV00008B/343